THE BIG
STING

The True Story
of the Canadian who
Betrayed Colombia's Drug Barons

THE BIG
STING

PETER EDWARDS

Based on Exclusive Interviews with Douglas Jaworski

KEY PORTER BOOKS

Canadian Cataloguing in Publication Data

Edwards, Peter, 1956-
        The Big Sting

ISBN 1-55013-360-8

1. Narcotics, Control of—Canada.   2. Jaworski, Douglas.
3. Royal Canadian Mounted Police.
I. Title.

HV5840.C3E38 1991   363.4'5'0971   C91-094508-X

Key Porter Books Limited
70 The Esplanade
Toronto, Ontario
Canada M5E 1R2

Printed and bound in Canada
91 92 93 94 95 6 5 4 3 2 1

CONTENTS

PREFACE

INFORMER DOUG JAWORSKI MADE INNUMER-
able suggestions on how to outmanoeuvre the Medellin cocaine cartel while he was working with the Royal Canadian
Mounted Police on the biggest drug sting in Canadian history.
But he was not in a position to make demands. The same
source-handler situation was true for these pages. Jaworski was
interviewed extensively for this book. He read drafts of the
manuscript, gave suggestions and corrected factual errors. But
I retained total editorial control over the final product.

The project was often a disturbing one. Like his Mountie
handlers, I often wondered how someone from a comfortable
home who seemed to be a nice guy could also have been
involved with a murderous organization like the Medellin
cartel. Writing this book has helped me probe this question.
Like his Mountie handlers, I found Jaworski to be truthful, if
unrepentant. Also, like his Mountie friends, I sometimes found
myself speculating and worrying about his future. If he can
keep his head down for the next five years, I feel he will
probably be safe. I am not totally convinced he can do this,
but I certainly hope he can. While I do not like many of the
things he has done or believes, I still like him as a person.

Whatever his motives for becoming involved in the sting,
neither his friends nor his enemies, either inside or outside the
police, can deny that Doug Jaworski has had an impact--in
drug interdiction strategies, in knowledge of inner workings
of the cartel, and in police handling of informers. Doug
Jaworski woke up Canada to the world of big league, globalized
drug trafficking. What's done with that knowledge remains to
be seen.

I have not shied away from criticizing Jaworski in these pages. I think he is an interesting and significant man, but the word hero does not apply. He candidly agrees with this.

The only area I have held back concerns the security of Doug Jaworski and his family. As I complete the book, he is beginning his new life, which I hope will be a long and legal one. I do not know details of his new life and I do not wish to know. Such knowledge might affect his security as well as my own. *The Big Sting* is intended to be an honest, often harsh examination of Douglas Jaworski's involvement with what is probably the world's richest and most dangerous narcotics trafficking group. It is not a roadmap for any new cartel hit-team. The seriousness of the threat to Jaworski was underlined by the murder of lawyer Sydney Leithman in May 1991, when the book was in its final stages of preparation.

All conversations quoted in the book are from either verbatim wiretaps or the memories of participants. The same applies to descriptions.

A number of people helped out. My thanks to Inspector Wayne Blackburn, Lee Davis Creal, Richard Duplain, Michael Fisher, Sergeant Mark Fleming, Superintendent Wayne Frechette, Jennifer Glossop, Joe Hall, Darcy Henton, Reg and Maureen Jaworski, Corporal Reg King, Lee Lamothe, Inspector William Lenton, Carol Lindsay, Sergeant Bob Lowe, Staff Sergeant Allan MacDonald, Lori MacDonald, Corporal Len McMaster, Corporal Keith Milner (who supplied the image of Jaworski as a chameleon), Eloise Morin, Antonio Nicaso, Corporal Daniel Paradis, Sergeant Guy Quintal, Rob Rueter, Richard Starck, Sergeant Wayne Umansky, David Vienneau, Inspector Don Willett, and, as always and most importantly, Lori, Sarah and James.

— P.E.

CAST OF CHARACTERS

THE JAWORSKIS

Douglas — a.k.a. Daniel. Canadian aviation expert who sold aircraft to the Medellin cocaine cartel and became high-level informer for the Royal Canadian Mounted Police.

Maureen — mother of Doug and former operator of sail cruise business in British Virgin Islands.

Reg — Maureen's husband and former partner in British Virgin Islands cruise business, Doug's father, and former senior Air Canada pilot.

Susan — Doug's wife, who finally left him in mid-1989.

THE POLICE

Toronto

Constable Pat Akin — Monitored bugs in Montreal sting.

Inspector Wayne Blackburn — head of operations for RCMP Toronto drug squad and key mastermind of Operation Overstep, the sting of Medellin cartel members in Canada.

Constable Bert Gillies — first Mountie to talk to Doug Jaworski about his defection plan.

Sergeant Bob Lowe — Toronto drug squad veteran and constant companion of Doug Jaworski during sting.

Staff Sergeant Allan MacDonald — Toronto drug squad leader who was with case from start to finish.

Lori MacDonald — former staff member of Toronto RCMP who worked on case from start to finish. No relation to Staff Sergeant MacDonald.

Corporal Keith Milner — Gillies' former boss, who met Doug Jaworski at Pearson International Airport and reassured him

11

that becoming an informer was the right thing to do. Key Jaworski handler.

Corporal Varouj Pogharian — former undercover Mountie. Spanish-speaking.

Sergeant Wayne Umansky — Toronto drug squad undercover ace. Constantly with Jaworski throughout sting.

Inspector Don Willett — became Blackburn's immediate superior after sting and before court cases.

Inspector Doug Ewing — one of operation's architects. Particularly important in Albany, N.Y. end of operation.

Montreal

Inspector William Lenton — Inspector Blackburn's Montreal equivalent.

Corporal Daniel Paradis — liaison between RCMP and Crown prosecutors. Worked into the ground.

Sergeant Guy Quintal — a key Montreal figure in sting. Unofficially best-dressed Mountie in Canada.

New Brunswick

Sergeant Mark Fleming — involved in both sting operation and investigation into attempted jail breakout.

Corporal Len McMaster — undercover operator who entertained cartel pilots in Toronto.

THE CARTEL
Colombia

Alejandro Diego Vasquez Caycedo — a.k.a. Diego Caycedo, Mauricio, Mauro. Doug Jaworski's former boss and friend, in charge of aviation for Medellin cocaine cartel. His responsibilities included creating new drug routes for cartel.

Fausto Caycedo — a.k.a. Joseph Diego's younger brother.

Pablo Emilio Escobar-Gaviria — a.k.a. God, the Pope, Peter.

Diego Caycedo's boss, a former hitman and headstone thief, now widely considered the richest criminal in the world. Key figure in Medellin cartel, which is believed to handle 80 percent of cocaine coming into North America. Referred to in this book as Pablo Escobar, the name by which he is most commonly known.

Carlos Enrique Lehder-Rivas — top cartel figure and founder now imprisoned in United States. Referred to in this book as Carlos Lehder.

Galiano — has airplane parts firm in Colombia.

The Doctor — real name unknown. Rival of Caycedo's.

United States

Eduardo Martinez Romero — financial wizard for cartel now jailed in U.S. Referred to in this book as Eduardo Martinez.

Frank — cartel figure in Florida. Early Doug Jaworski contact and business rival. Referred to in book as Frank the gofer.

Sonny — a.k.a. William Robinson, Floyd Vaughn. Pilot. Fugitive from police.

Ron Whitaker — worker for Sonny.

Diego Jose Ganuza— a.k.a. Masters. Cuban pilot.

Roberto Striedinger — a.k.a. Streidinger, Striendinger, Steiner. Florida pilot and rich businessman.

Sedenio —copilot for 1989 flight into Quebec.

Canada

Richard Delgado-Marquez — a.k.a. John. Cartel Montreal distribution team.

Flor Emilse Mery-Correa — Cartel Montreal distribution team member. Said to be romantically involved with Pablo Escobar.

Fernando William Mendoza-Salazar — a.k.a. Carlos Mario Ortega Gonzales. Cartel Montreal distribution member.

Albin Geovanny Mery-Correa — Flor Emilse Mery-Correa's brother. Arrested in Toronto end of sting.

Beatriz Pelez — arrested in Toronto end of sting.

Jose Ali Galindo-Escobar — a.k.a. Jay. Senior cartel pilot, relative of Pablo Escobar, and friend of Diego Caycedo. Referred to in this book as Jay.

Fernando Augusto Mendoza-Jaramillo — a.k.a. Pinguino. Jay's copilot. Referred to in this book by nickname of Pinguino.

Julio Cesar Bracho-Sucre — a.k.a. Jaird Perez Rodriguez, William Jose Rodriguez, Ricardo Marin, Alexander Galindo-Escovar. M-19 guerrilla and leader of team that tried to break cartel pilots out of Fredericton jail.

Luis Felipe Briceno-Leon — a.k.a. Wilmer Ramon Zanabria-Bueno, Jorge Alcides Mendoza-Angarita. M-19 guerrilla and member of team that tried to break cartel pilots out of Fredericton jail.

Jose Eulogio Manzano-Bustamante — a.k.a. Fredy Omar Fuenamyor Matute, Eulojio Manzano. M-19 guerrilla and member of team that tried to break cartel pilots out of Fredericton jail.

Juan Carlos Hernandez — a.k.a. Oswaldo Jose Gonzalez-Tineo, J. Garcia, Miguel Angel Castrillo-Dudasmel. M-19 guerrilla and member of team that tried to break cartel pilots out of Fredericton jail.

Roberto Ambrosio San Vicente Freitas — a.k.a. Roberto San Vicente, Tito Sanchez-Ruiz, Roberto Sanvincente. Former Toronto resident. Convicted with Maritime breakout squad. Nicknamed "The Accidental Terrorist," because of his denial he knew anything about plot to break cartel pilots out of Fredericton jail.

OFFICERS OF THE COURT

Madame Justice Claire Barrette-Joncas — Quebec Superior Court judge. Heard closed-doors case on Jaworski family's security in February 1990 after Supreme Court of Canada decision.

Justice Jacques Ducros — experienced judge who tried Montreal distribution team.

Provincial Court Judge James Harper — tried Colombian squad which attempted New Brunswick jail break.

Sydney Leithman — lawyer for member of cartel Montreal distribution team and pilot Diego Jose Ganuza. Had represented many underworld figures.

Jacques Malboeuf — Montreal prosecutor.

Julio Peris — Montreal lawyer who represented member of Montreal cocaine distribution team.

Maximilien Polak — judge for Ganuza trial.

Robert Rueter — Jaworski's Toronto lawyer.

Richard Starck — Montreal prosecutor for trials of Montreal distribution teams and Ganuza.

Jack Waissman — Montreal lawyer who represented member of Montreal cocaine distribution team.

THE BIG STING

1/ PEARSON INTERNATIONAL AIRPORT

"It was just a matter of being able to play my cards right."

— Douglas Jaworski

RCMP CONSTABLE BERT GILLIES WAS WORKING at Pearson International Airport shortly before noon on Friday, December 16, 1988, when a young man with a deep tan showed up to tell a wild story. Airport police receive almost daily visits from people needing psychiatric, not police, help. But this stranger was intriguing and seemed rational, if extremely nervous.

At 12:15, Gillies placed a call to his supervisor, Corporal Keith Milner.

"Listen, would you come over to Terminal 2?" Gillies asked. "I've got someone here that I'd like you to speak to."

"Is it really necessary?" Milner replied. He was working through lunch, trying to get through a mound of paperwork that was part of the new job he had taken after leaving the Toronto drug section of the Mounties.

Gillies pressed on.

"I don't want to go into it over the phone. Come on over here. You're going to be very interested when you get here."

When he got to the Terminal 2 interview room fifteen minutes later, Gillies took Milner aside.

"Look, there's a fellow who walked in here. He started talking to me and he's talked for about three-quarters of an hour about high-level dope dealers from South America. I've never done drug work so I'd really appreciate it if you go in and figure out just who he is and see if he's bona fide."

Milner's first observation was that Doug Jaworski was not dressed for December in Toronto. He was sitting in an interview office, wearing a blue knit polo sweater, acid-wash blue jeans, Italian Fila running shoes, a gold Rolex watch, and Ray-Ban sunglasses. His hair was stylishly cut, and he sported a rich tan that was clearly not from a booth or a quick trip to Florida.

When Milner asked Jaworski to take off his Ray-Bans, he refused. When Milner asked why, Jaworski replied simply, "I don't want to take the sunglasses off."

Jaworski's voice was almost a falsetto. He sat slouched in his chair with his hands in his lap. His fingers were intertwined, and he twiddled his thumbs nervously. He didn't look like an international dope dealer; he looked more like a boy-next-door from a rich neighborhood, someone who would have trouble growing a beard.

But Jaworski seemed to be for real. He explained to Milner that he could help the Mounties nab key members of the Medellin cocaine cartel, which imported an estimated 80 percent of the cocaine on North American streets and was widely considered the world's most vicious criminal enterprise. Milner had heard that informers against the cartel were often executed by means of a "Colombian necktie." Their throats were slit vertically and their tongues yanked out in front of their eyes in a piece of lethal and bloody symbolism. Often, informers' entire families were slaughtered as a warning to others. If Jaworski was telling the truth, his nervousness was understandable. If not, then this kid liked to lie on a grand scale.

Whenever Milner pressed him for specifics, Jaworski tightened up. "That's another story," he'd reply. The two sides were measuring each other, in the police equivalent of a courtship dance.

"I'm going to have to get some concrete information," Milner said. "I'm prepared to take you to see my boss and tell him that I think you're bona fide, but only if you can give me some concrete details."

Jaworski obliged with some information about cartel plans to bring drugs into Canada with Turbo Commander and Beach King-Air executive airplanes. When he talked of drug routes, he gave exact flight coordinates, but it was clear he still did not trust Milner.

"I want you to call me at the office," Milner said.

"I'm going away with my wife," Jaworski replied. "We're going on a bit of a holiday over the Christmas break. I'll call you when I've had some time to be with my wife."

Afraid he might lose him, Milner kept pressing. "Why are you doing this? There's got to be a reason that you want to get out."

"Yeah, there is. I have to get out. I have some problems, but basically if I stay in, my problems are going to multiply. Right now I have a choice. I either get out by helping you people and clearing myself up with any problems I might have, or I have to take off for Europe or somewhere else in the world. I have a complete set of identification in another name. I can basically set myself up as someone else. I can probably live out the rest of my days, but my wife would never go along with that. I haven't really talked that over with her at all. But I don't think that she'd be ready to go along with that. So do I present her with that or do I present her with the fact that I've done these things and I want to get out and now I'm going to work it out and start all over again?"

"Look, I want you to call me. This is my office number," Milner replied.

Jaworski still seemed to be somewhere far away.

"Here's my home telephone number," Milner said, knowing he was stepping outside regular bounds. "If I'm not there when you call, then Andrea, my wife, will take the call. I'll tell her that I'm expecting a call from a guy named Doug that's very important. When she gets that call, she'll get to me any way she can."

Jaworski looked up. Once again he was attentive. "You'd give me your wife's name and your home telephone number? Well, if you can trust me that far, then I'll trust you."

Milner noted the sunglasses were off now. The Mountie later recalled, "It was like the barrier came down. The glasses came off, and I saw Doug Jaworski for the first time."

Milner pressed the advantage. "Before you go, I need some concrete details."

Suddenly, he had to scribble furiously to keep up as, for half an hour, Jaworski rattled off details of air routes, drug traffickers, and his tenure with the cartel.

Jaworski later recalled, "I was testing the waters to see if it was possible. Milner basically brought me into his confidence. I liked him and I trusted him. I wanted to like him and I wanted to trust him, so it made it easier for me to do it. I wanted a receptive officer."

On the flight north to Canada, he had been nervous that the police might not take him seriously. He wanted to hook the Mounties, but also keep his bargaining power. For the past six months, he had been mentally rehearsing how to approach police. He knew it would take a little work to ensure his credibility. "Put yourself in the position of an RCMP officer who has a little kid coming in and saying he's going to help you with the biggest drug bust that Canada has ever heard of. I only gave him bits of information so that he could do his checks.... I didn't give them enough information to do a case without me.... I knew that I had something more valuable than they had ever had in this country. I knew that. It was just a matter of being able to play my cards right."

Jaworski not only liked Milner, he had more trust in Canadian law enforcement officers than in their American counterparts. "I did think that the RCMP was better than the DEA (American Drug Enforcement Administration) because the DEA had so many dirty cops. I hadn't heard of a dirty RCMP drug cop and I didn't think that the cartel was that well entrenched in Canada to get dirty cops."

Just in case there were problems with Mountie security, Jaworski approached them with a plan that he thought would take only a month to complete. The cartel was already moving and the trap had to be sprung quickly if it was going to work. "I thought that approaching the RCMP a month before would be about right," Jaworski later recalled. "If I went a week before, it wouldn't be enough time, and if I went three months before, the word would have spread so bad that I would have been overexposed. If there had been a bad apple [in the RCMP], I would have been fucked."

Jaworski found Milner likable and interested, but also calm and somewhat guarded. "I expected him to get a little more excited," Jaworski later said. But he walked out of Pearson airport feeling positive about the meeting, although still nervous. "All I needed was to make one tiny mistake. It didn't have to be a big one. Just a tiny one.... If I fucked up, I knew I'd be a statistic."

Even if Jaworski couldn't read it on his face, Milner was excited. When Jaworski left, Milner felt as if he had just grabbed a tiger by the tail. Drug officers always joke about hitting the elusive mother lode or uncovering a huge stash of drugs, and this case had the potential to be the kind that can make a career. But corporals cannot set RCMP policy, and now Milner had to sell the case at a higher level.

After praising Gillies for spotting the case's possibilities, Milner headed off to see his own superior, Staff Sergeant Mark Porter. Porter suggested they pass it on to Superintendent Larry Proke, who was in charge of security at Pearson International and who had previously handled the Clifford Olson child murders case.

"I've got a feeling that Jaworski is what he says he is," Milner told Proke, "and he can do what he says he can do on our behalf."

Proke was receptive but thought that the case was too big for him. "You just came from the Toronto drug squad," he told Milner. "Why don't you go downtown and see Inspector Doug Ewing?"

Milner called Ewing, and by the time he arrived downtown, Ewing, administration officer in charge of the drug section, had assembled a half dozen top drug officers.

Before Jaworski approached the Mounties, drug officers in Canada had already forecast a scenario like the one Jaworski had outlined to Milner, where the cartel flies cocaine north to Canada's maritime coastline, then ships the narcotic south again to the United States. But not everyone believed the thirteen-hour plane flight was possible for a small airplane, and it was common knowledge that police corruption in Mexico made it a well-traveled conduit for American-bound drugs.

Now Milner had information that drugs were coming directly into Canada, and he was offering the Mounties a crack at the upper echelons of the largest cocaine-smuggling operation in the world.

Ewing responded to the news by asking Milner what he was doing the next few months. Suddenly Milner was back on the drug squad. Airport work had much saner, more regular hours than drug enforcement, but this case seemed so full of potential that Milner didn't want to simply be a messenger boy.

He could feel a surge of adrenalin as Inspector Wayne Blackburn, operations manager for the drug squad, told him to start drawing up a file on Jaworski. Blackburn had a reputation for supporting his men in the field and for liking detailed reports, so that new officers could step into a case and get up to speed quickly. He could have had no idea how the case would affect his career and his life when he told Milner, "I want everything on paper."

For the Mounties, the case offered an entry into the cartel through the front door as well as a record bust in terms of volume. Normally, police pose as drug buyers and try to work their way up the organization. Now, they would be starting at the top. If they did a sting, they would be the ones with the drugs. It was a total reversal of roles, which Blackburn later likened to trying to tie up your shoes by using a mirror.

That Sunday, Milner locked himself in his den from seven in the morning until eight at night. When he emerged, he had fourteen pages of details about Jaworski, his cartel boss Diego Caycedo, the cartel's safehouses, planes, bodyguards, and plans for Canada.

Now all they needed was a call back from Jaworski.

2/ THE CHAMELEON

"The chameleon's dish: I eat the air, promise-crammed."

— William Shakespeare, *Hamlet*

THE MEDELLIN CARTEL SELDOM LOOKS TO outsiders for assistance, except for help from money-launderers and pilots. By his mid-twenties, Doug Jaworski could fill the bill on both counts. He also looked young for his age and, with his boyish charm, could manipulate people into giving him what he sought. That skill he honed early in life.

Doug's father was a senior Air Canada pilot and his mother a nurse-turned-homemaker. The family moved a lot, from a 100-acre farm outside Ottawa, to comfortable homes in Hamilton, Orillia, and Georgetown, Ontario, to Ste. Adèle, Quebec, and to Washington State. The moves came about every second year, but Jaworski would later say that he never had trouble moving or adjusting to his new homes. He's not sure why this is true but he knows that it is. And he can understand why he might be compared to a chameleon, even though the association to a cold-blooded reptile is not appealing.

His parents, Reg and Maureen, say he was a well-behaved, pleasant, fairly unremarkable youngster who was never so much as sent home from school for misbehaving. Reg later recalled, "He never really stood out when he was a kid. I never really noticed him. Of course, I wasn't home that much because of the employment that I was in.... I was probably away from home as much as two-thirds of the month. When I did get home, I was tired, so the responsibility fell mostly to Maureen."

But Reg Jaworski did help his son develop his skills with people. "Doug's very quick to catch on to things.... When he was a youngster, before he was even going to school, we were sitting out in the back yard and he said, 'Dad, I want a cookie.' I said, 'If you want a cookie, what I suggest you do is go to your mother and ask her for a kiss. And then ask her for a cookie.' So of course, that's what he did. What is she going to do? He was able to realize that if you compliment someone and then ask them for something, it works easy that way."

Like a chameleon, Jaworski was inordinately adept at avoiding battles, not winning them. Jaworski later said he cannot ever remember getting into fights while growing up, despite repeated taunts from another boy in grades nine and ten in Orillia. Even as a child, he preferred flight over fighting. "Every time that there was tension, I'd avoid the conflict, walk away. There was this kid in high school who always wanted to fight me. I never figured out if he was jealous or what.... I used to avoid him. If I saw him walking down the hall, I'd go the other way."

Doug Jaworski was a strong if often bored student and dropped out of high school after his family moved to Washington State, even though he needed only a credit in

American history for graduation. The prospect of spending a year taking just one course was unappealing. Instead Jaworski dropped out, passed a high school equivalency test, and left home.

First, there was a job in Toronto developing film for school pictures, which Jaworski recalled with disgust. "I could take it for only a week. It was terrible. No window to look out or anything. It was the worst week of my life, dark all the time." Then he was off to work as a runner on the Chicago commodities exchange, staying at the home of a relative who was living there. He loved this job because of the market's intrigue. "It's a bunch of guys yelling and screaming at each other all day long. I was like a nobody. My particular role there, as a sixteen-year-old, was so low that it would have been a promotion if I got a broom to sweep the floor. I was in the most menial starting position. My thing was to take little pieces of paper to the guys who screamed and waved their hands and to pick little pieces of paper up off the floor and bring them back to the desk after the order was filled. It intrigued me because I didn't know anything about it. What you learn is completely dependent on how much you want to learn. I felt that school was very restrictive. But on the stock exchange, sometimes I carried millions of dollars. An order of 100,000 bushels of wheat at $7 a bushel is $700,000. It didn't mean anything. It was just numbers."

When he was only seventeen, his parents bought him a $20,000 Cessna airplane so he could learn to fly. At the same time, they were moving to the Caribbean, to set up a business offering sailing cruises to tourists. With his new plane, Jaworski moved to Florida, where the sunny weather meant he could be airborne every day. He flourished on his own, earning his commercial pilot's license within a year, then selling the plane and repaying his parents. Flight meant freedom and Jaworski was not modest about his abilities.

"I like flying alone and I like flying on long trips and going to different spots. I like flying South American routes and African routes and the North Atlantic. I love flying over Greenland and Iceland. There's always something different. It was something I could do on my own and I didn't have to answer to anybody. To fly for an airline is very regimented. But when you're flying for yourself in a private airplane, you get to do whatever you want.

"Would I enjoy the tension of flying in a war? I doubt it. It would be fun to fly an F-18 and go straight up in the air at the speed of sound. But other than that, I don't think I'd want to put up with the discipline that the military would make you deal with.

"I don't like tinkering with a plane. I'm not a mechanic, but I can usually fix it if I have to. But I don't enjoy doing it. I don't like getting my hands dirty like that.

"I hated school. I loved flying and I aced that. That's all the school that I've had. I'm a great pilot. I wouldn't make a great teacher but I'm a great pilot. I wanted to go to the top fast. I was a good pilot but I wasn't a safe pilot. If it started, I flew it, and if it had a problem, I dealt with it."

And no matter how fast or far he traveled, there seemed to be no real danger, as long as his hands were on the controls.

3/ THE SOURCE

"He looked at it as some kind of death machine."

— A Bolivian soldier looks at an aircraft flown by
Douglas Jaworski.

THEY STARED AT DOUG JAWORSKI AS IF HE WERE
from another world. Deep in the northern Bolivian jungle, far
from roads, electricity, or television, the native family had
never before seen anyone quite like him. "They were afraid of
me at first," Jaworski said. "They had never seen anybody with
blue eyes. I scared the bejesus out of them. They would just
stare. I felt they were looking at me like I was from outer
space."

Jaworski had just dropped off a Cessna 206 at an airstrip in
the Beni region of northern Bolivia. His customer invited
him to spend the night at a remote farm he owned before
putting Jaworski on a commercial flight in Santa Cruz, destined
back to Florida.

Everything about the place was an adventure for Jaworski.
The skins of two ocelots were drying in the sun, and he

counted seventeen parrots in a tree. The farmers were trying to kill another ocelot in an effort to guard their pigs. To do this, they shot a monkey, tied it on a stake, and then hid and waited for the big cat to arrive.

At night, the natives hunted from the dugout by slowly cruising the shoreline. Flashlights were taped to their gun barrels, and their eyes were trained on the shoreline. "It was neat," Jaworski recalled. "Whatever reflected light, you shot it. Animals' eyes reflect light. Like with a deer. When you're driving your car, you see its eyes first." The jungle was so dense and so remote that there was little chance of blasting a passerby by mistake. Jaworski also fished for piranha from the dugout canoe. Always ready for new sensations, he discovered that barbecued piranha tasted a lot like bass.

The region had known a brief boom of prosperity a century before when Europeans came to make their fortunes in the rubber trade. It was said that some of these early visitors were so rich and so leery of jungle waters that they sent their laundry back to Europe for cleaning. But eventually these rubber barons left, and the jungle took over again.

By the 1980s, the harvest was no longer rubber: it was now coca. On the farm Jaworski visited was a small lab for processing cocaine paste.

Much of the coca came from nearby farms. The coca for some 30 to 40 percent of the world's cocaine was cultivated in the Chapare valley rain forest. The region's 300,000 residents were almost all engaged in coca production, and most had migrated to the region after the market for coca — and its byproduct, cocaine — accelerated in the 1970s as cocaine became a symbol of disposable wealth and conspicuous consumption in North America.

Processing cocaine is an extremely technical and dangerous job, since the ingredients involved are all extremely volatile. The best chemicals are from Germany and arrive in South

American ports via ships. From there, they are often transported inland on tanker trucks like the ones used to move gasoline in North America. Officials along the entire transportation network are paid off to make sure the cargo moves smoothly.

Ironically, some of the most sophisticated cocaine operations used the most remote locations for their labs. Airstrips were closely watched by the military but helicopters could deposit their cargo on small farms far removed from prying eyes.

Labs were not impressive to look at. They were usually either in the open or in rundown sheds, areas with no one nearby to complain of the nauseating stench of the vapor from the toxic brew of coca paste, ether, hydrochloric acid, and acetone. It was not uncommon for cooks to be killed when their labs blew up. The successful and lucky ones took on a ghostly shade of gray as the vapor reacted with their skin. To test the purity of the product, they dropped a piece of Clorox bleach into the bubbling pot. If the stuff was of high quality, the surface of the brew would soon be covered with a yellowish and oily film. Once done, the product was left to dry either in the sun or, in an urban area, under a sunlamp. Then it was off to the ever-hungry markets of North America at price markups that could hit 1,000 percent.

In 1980, the United States government had shut off all foreign aid to the junta that ruled Bolivia, after it received reports that government officers were deeply involved in the drug trade. Food aid resumed shortly afterwards amid promises that the Bolivian government would combat coca cultivation and move toward civilian rule.

In an effort to fight the cocaine trade, Bolivian government agronomists tried to convince farmers to cultivate black pepper, macadamia nuts, coconuts, ginger, and other crops in the place of coca bushes. Farmers were paid to destroy their coca harvests, and many did so, then planted a new coca crop. Food for their families came first, and coca yielded four crops a year from harsh mountain slopes and required little cultivation. Farmers also knew they would always have a market for the crop, and they nicknamed the thin, sparse bushes "oro verde" or green gold.

In their native culture, coca was not foreign or threatening. Since Incan times, Bolivians have sucked on coca leaves, sometimes mixing them with lime, to gain release from hunger, thirst, fatigue, and the cold. Highland fortune tellers used the leaves for tea and religious offerings. Natives, however, had been able to control their uses of the leaf and had never refined or consumed the highly addictive strains of cocaine popular in North America.

At the jungle farm, Jaworski found nothing like the paranoia and mania for power that he would come to associate with the cocaine trade. "That whole big drug dealer atmosphere was absent. You have to understand that you are hundreds of miles from anything. You go out there and there's this family. You can tell they're a family. They are not cut-throat gangsters, but just a family of paisanos. There was nothing threatening about them, other than that the husband wore a pistol like a cowboy. But he didn't wear it because they were afraid of anybody coming out. It was more for animals."

By the 1980s, the drug trade offered Bolivia both the promise and the threat of an economic boom reminiscent of the days of the rubber barons. The vehicle for this new wealth was the Cessna 206, nicknamed the "Bolivian Special." A used model cost about $60,000 (U.S.) and a brand-new one about $105,000. Either offered the hope of fortunes. Slow-moving station wagons of the air, the Cessnas were capable of holding three forty-five-gallon barrels of ether or kerosene. Drug traders used them for transporting heavy loads of coca paste from Bolivia or Peru, for picking up coca leaves in Bolivia's granary, the Cochabamba region, or for transporting chemicals such as ether from Brazil.

During the early 1980s, it was common for drug traffickers to work their Cessnas until they were little more than scrap. Then they would tie the tail of an aircraft to a tree, rev the engine up to full power, slash the line, and watch the plane smash into trees and explode. At this point, all it took was a call to Lloyd's of London and a sad tale about faulty fuel and a disastrous takeoff before the owner could collect money for a new plane.

Insurance companies eventually became wiser and stopped issuing coverage. Always innovative, traffickers then began sending bundles of mashed aluminum aircraft parts to Florida, ostensibly for repair. A new aircraft would be delivered and a paid-off government inspector would attest that this was merely a rebuilt version of the old parts. With this, traffickers could dodge high tariffs on aircraft imports. Officials could always be tricked, bought off, or eliminated.

By the early 1980s, Jaworski was busy delivering planes south to Bolivia. He expected strange experiences in these flights and got them. At night, the world seemed upside down, with the stars above him offering light while the world below was total darkness. But everything about one particular flight seemed a bit odd even for his tastes. While all his customers wanted their planes, these buyers seemed a little too anxious. When he stopped en route from Florida to Bolivia in Trinidad and opened up a loose panel to fix binding wire in the floor, Jaworski discovered why.

"I found the whole plane was packed with money — stuffed to the wings. It was mostly tens and twenties. When you get those small bills, it's crack [cocaine] money. I called the buyers on the phone and I said, 'Okay, you bastards, you've been using me. I don't know for how long, but you're going to start to pay. If you want this airplane, I want fifteen grand.' They said, 'Yes, yes! We didn't tell you we were doing it because we thought you might steal it from us.'"

Jaworski's commission suddenly rose from $3,000 to $15,000 for the three-day trip. He made about fifteen more of these flights, then invested his money in a Fort Lauderdale area airplane sales and repair shop. The new fee was no major loss for his Bolivian clients, since each plane held about a million dollars cash and the owners' commission for smuggling the money was 10 percent or $100,000. "Everybody was happy for the longest time," Jaworski said. "That's how a lot of money is taken out of Miami."

Some schemes he heard about had more finesse. One Bolivian investor favored by drug traffickers began giving a 14 percent return on investments. Word spread about his money-making abilities, and more and more drug traffickers laundered their profits through him. For this, they received computerized statements telling them how quickly their wealth was multiplying. One day, he vanished, along with some $32 million in drug money. Victims were powerless, since they couldn't run to authorities without raising suspicions. "Everybody was crying about it," Jaworski recalled. "Of course, everybody said they lost $10 million when they probably had only $300,000 in there with him. They never found him. I thought it was hilarious."

At first, Jaworski felt helpless in Bolivia, as he bribed government officials to let him go about his business. But soon his trips there became routine, as was wearing his cowboy boots or refueling planes with buckets at tiny airports. "If you go to South America, take a whole wad of brand-new currency in one-dollar bills," Jaworski later said. "Just hand them out as you go along. That's the only way. People get all excited because it's new. The money in the jungle is so tattered and worn that most of it's ready to fall apart."

Even when he wasn't passing out crisp one-dollar bills, people appeared happy to see him. To drug dealers, his arrival meant they would get the aircraft they so badly wanted. To the local women, he brought an aura of American wealth, opportunity, and glamour. His nickname in Bolivia was Michael J. Fox, for the television and movie star.

Bolivia's economy was as volatile as the chemicals used to make cocaine. Jaworski once saw a room with bills piled to the ceiling, but the huge stack added up to only $100,000. The money's owner, Fernando Gutierrez, put a human face on this economic instability. Fernando was related to Alfredo Gutierrez, who had been driven from Florida after placing a murder contract on American undercover Drug Enforcement Administration agent Michael Levine. What detonated Gutierrez's rage was that he had delivered $5 million to Levine, thinking it was for a drug deal. To raise $1 million for bail, Gutierrez's private airstrip had to be mortgaged, and when Gutierrez fled America, the family was suddenly without money or its source of income.

Alberto Gutierrez was as big as a pro football lineman, weighing in in the neighborhood of 270 pounds. But, without his airstrip, he suddenly became a sad figure around the Santa Cruz airport. Jaworski recalled, "He was like a fallen benefactor, a guy that you could tell used to have a lot of money and didn't have any now. He was just grappling around, trying to figure out how to hit the big time again."

At one point, Jaworski knew Alberto wanted something from him, but he couldn't figure out what it was. The Bolivian appeared eager to buy a $3-million plane. But Jaworski's Spanish was poor, as was the drug dealer's English. Finally, it was explained to Jaworski what Gutierrez really wanted to do: steal an aircraft, fly it full of cocaine to Europe, then drop off the drugs, and resell the plane. For this, the drug dealer would let Jaworski split the profits, but not until after the deal. Jaworski declined and later laughed at the notion of taking all the risks and then splitting the profits. "I got hundreds of offers," he said.

With Fernando Gutierrez, Jaworski never quite knew what was real, other than Fernando's ambition to raise his family to the level of its past affluence. That naturally meant cocaine trafficking. Fernando constantly carried the newspaper obituary of a young friend who had died of cancer. Fernando solemnly told Jaworski he had promised his friend on his deathbed that he would carry the obituary when he completed his first major dope deal. Cocaine trafficking became an almost holy mission for Fernando, who seemed intoxicated by his dreams. Fernando lied, even when he didn't have to, and he was always trying to cast himself as a character of epic proportions. He didn't just want to smuggle cocaine; he wanted the biggest cocaine empire in the world. He had good connections — his uncle was high up in the Bolivian air force — but it was difficult for a Bolivian like Fernando to make it to the top of the cocaine world. The country was landlocked and isolated, too far from the American market for direct flights. Its northern neighbor, Colombia, had a northern ocean coastline and ports on two oceans. The Colombians had better access to America by air. Life was easier for them.

As much as they hated the notion, men like Fernando were forced to deal with Colombians to the north. When Jaworski heard talk in Santa Cruz about Colombian drug barons, it was laced with an underdog's resentment and hatred, with the Colombians painted as cheats even by criminal standards.

Other drug dealers were forced to resort to bizarre, bold schemes to sneak cocaine into the United States. Women were sent north with cocaine strapped to their bodies, in custom-made bras and girdles. It came north in platform shoes, wooden legs, and in the bellies of couriers who risked their lives by swallowing condoms full of the narcotic. The strangest ploy Jaworski heard about involved Peruvian traffickers who hollowed out the corpse of a young boy, stuffed it with cocaine, and shipped it north to the United States in a casket, ostensibly for a decent burial.

Jaworski learned not to be surprised or shocked by such occurrences. One day, Fernando Gutierrez opened a closet in his Santa Cruz villa and pulled out a wooden box. Proudly, he showed Jaworski his Nazi memorabilia, including an old machine gun and rusty grenades. They were gifts from Nazi fugitive and war criminal Klaus Barbie, "The Butcher of Lyons," Fernando said. Barbie had some influence in the government after the 1980 "cocaine coup," when a relative of Roberto Suarez, the King of Cocaine, became interior minister.

Roberto Suarez himself was not beyond grand gestures. He once published an open letter to U.S. president Ronald Reagan, offering to turn himself in if his son was released from custody in Florida and if the United States paid off the Bolivian national debt. The overture was rejected, but it was impressive nonetheless, as were his gold-plated handgun and the gold collar studded with diamonds that his pet leopard was said to wear. There were also Suarez's boasts that he had hired Libyan experts to train his security team and that missile-carrying aircraft guarded his ranch quarters in the Beni region. His popularity was said to come in large part because he gained his wealth through Yankee depravity rather than by robbing his native country.

The mountains of Bolivia were also alive with legends of spirits, like that of a giant condor who was the messenger of the sun and able to fly to the gods. During one flight, Jaworski heard a modern tale about events that had happened just a few days before his arrival and seemed certain to become a jungle legend. A Cessna 206 had become stuck on the heavy canopy of the jungle. It was too late in the day for a helicopter rescue. The next day, when a rescuer was lowered down to the aircraft from a helicopter, he saw two human skeletons, picked totally clean by ants. "That was a real rude awakening to just how bad the jungle was," Jaworski said. "The army guy was telling me about it. Just after it happened. He said, 'Oh, you're flying a 206.' He looked at it as some kind of death machine, besides the fact that it had three barrels of fuel in it that made it a bomb."

On Jaworski's first aircraft delivery to Bolivia, a spider the size of a steering wheel, with coarse hair all over its body, crawled out onto a jungle airstrip. Natives were first afraid, then taunted the huge insect.

"People who had lived their whole lives in the jungle had never seen anything like it," Jaworski said. "I hate spiders. It was about the ugliest thing I've ever seen in my life. They were used to seeing weird stuff in the jungle but this was extra weird."

Jaworski stared at it, disgusted and fascinated, but he did not read anything symbolic into it. Doug Jaworski liked to talk about how individuals control their own destiny. He did not believe in omens.

4/ BABYLON

"I had never seen a guy so scared in my life."

— Douglas Jaworski describes a business associate who ran
afoul of a cocaine baron.

HANS STRIEDINGER WAS IN A PANIC AND
desperately wanted his friend Doug Jaworski to help. Hans
had had his family's home in Key Biscayne, Florida, to himself.
There had been a party, and now the place was a mess. And his
father was due home anytime. Countless university-age youths
experience this anxiety, but it was tough to compare Hans
Striedinger with other people. For Hans, things were always
extreme and strange. His latest crisis began while he was
sharing a hot tub with a girl and another couple. Drugs had
been consumed. Then came the sex. Then partners were
swapped and another tryst in the warm water was enjoyed.
Afterwards, it was sleep, awash on waves of chemicals and
bubbling, Jacuzzied water. When Hans awoke, he found to his
horror that he had left the water running in the second-floor

hot tub and it had overflowed and poured down onto a lower floor. The ceiling had collapsed and damage was extensive.

Hans's father, Roberto, was particularly proud of the house. It had belonged to former American president Richard M. Nixon, and Nixon's first name and that of his wife, Pat, still appeared under hooks in the bath-house by the swimming pool. Roberto Striedinger loved to brag that he wrote a cheque for the $1-million deposit on the mansion just ten minutes after seeing it for the first time. "When I first saw this place, I fell in love with it," he would say. He said it cost him roughly $5 million, although authorities later set its worth at $2.6 million. Whatever the cost, it was more palace than house when he bought it. And since then, Roberto Striedinger had pumped a considerable amount of money into renovations, including a grand elevator with see-through, Plexiglass walls.

And now Hans had screwed up again. Not too much was expected from Hans any more, but even he wasn't supposed to get too stoned to turn off an upstairs tap. Hans hated it when he disappointed his father, which was often. There was the time he left the Jet-Ski unlocked by the heliport and someone stole it. Or the year he was sixteen, when he totaled three cars. Hans liked to drive only Porsches, and his introduction to driving had been expensive and chemical-filled.

Now, Hans was pleading over the phone with his friend Doug Jaworski. "I've got to get this fixed up and I don't know how to do it," Hans said.

Jaworski didn't know how to help. Hans kept calling his buddies, pleading for someone to bail him out. No one could, and like most crises in Hans's life, this one simply passed. There was no flash of enlightenment, no effort to do things differently the next time, no pause to consider his actions from a dispassionate distance. Just a headlong stumble into another mess and mumbles about his bad luck.

Hans loved his father and his father loved him, but they

were two very different men. Hans was attractive, with a lean, muscular athlete's build and sharp-featured, Latin good looks, highlighted by cheekbones as sharp as cut diamonds. But there was something desperate too. "I remember Hans being really skittish. It was like he had the shakes, like an alcoholic has the shakes."

Roberto Striedinger had a totally different presence. He was a serious businessman who knew about control. He had a firm command of himself and others around him and was something of a legend in South Florida and Colombia. Authorities would charge that he had been chief pilot for Medellin cartel drug baron Pablo Escobar when Escobar was pulling himself out of the gutter into notoriety. Jaworski had heard that Roberto Striedinger had the gall to organize a strike among Escobar's pilots. Thanks to him, the story went, Escobar's drug couriers were now treated as something special. Pay was now high — $450,000 could be made for less than two days' work — and skilled pilots no longer had to do sweaty grunt jobs like loading and unloading heavy bundles of cocaine. Striedinger was fired for his labor activism, but that wasn't the point. He had won on the issue and, just as impressively, he had not been murdered. For Roberto Striedinger, there were plenty of other ways to make money.

He owned a 100,000-acre cattle farm about 100 miles south of Villa Vincencio, as well as a shrimp farm and hearts of palm business in Colombia. And his home in Bogota was a sight to behold, a monument under construction to his ability to stand up and shine in a hostile environment. Tall and narrow, it was six floors of marble and granite, hacked into a sloping mountainside. The first floor had a single-lane bowling alley with a gymnasium above that. On the third floor was a swimming pool with a retractable, sloping, clear, bullet-proof ceiling. The main quarters and garage were above that. On the fifth floor was the kitchen and living room, capped with bedrooms on the sixth floor. It was as grand as the Nixon home and was being created with Striedinger's own vision and guile.

Roberto Striedinger carried himself as a businessman, but authorities had a jaundiced view of the nature of his varied commercial interests. West German police suspected him of smuggling cocaine into Europe inside tins of costly hearts of palm. Assistant U.S. attorney Guy Lewis would say in court that "this man sits, eats, drinks, and sleeps with the cartel."

It costs money to guard and maintain a fortune. Striedinger had $40,000 worth of security cameras installed in the Key Biscayne home, and television monitors seemed to be everywhere. When police finally raided the place years later, they found eighteen weapons, including a pair of AK-47 rifles, an AR-15, Uzi pistol, and MAC-10. Only one gun wasn't fully loaded.

Two nasty Dobermans patrolled the Florida grounds, and a German shepherd attempted to guard the Bogota property, in the shadow of a watch tower Striedinger had installed. While in Colombia, Striedinger often traveled with a hefty man in his fifties, who, the story went, learned his fluent English in Los Angeles while working as a killer for hire. He left the U.S. for Bogota when authorities got too close.

Striedinger himself knew something about dodging pesky authorities. Police charged that he often misspelled his name as a ploy to dodge law enforcement computer checks. They thought he was really named Steiner and wanted to speak to him because cartel informer Max Mermelstein had dubbed him "the number one man in the United States" for cocaine trafficking.

An irony about Striedinger's grand homes was that his wife, Piedad, refused to stay in them. That was another source of worry and tension for Striedinger. Theirs was a strange relationship. Once, when Jaworski asked Hans about his parents' marriage, he was jolted by Hans's response: "They're friends on the surface. As a matter of fact, she gave him a gun for Christmas."

Jaworski and Roberto Striedinger met in December 1986. Striedinger pulled up to the aircraft dealership in his long black Mercedes with gold trim. With the millionaire was Frank, a nondescript gofer in his fifties, a dangerous but forgettable little man always under the control of others.

They wanted Jaworski's help getting a Gulfstream Commander Jetprop 1000 out of the United States and into Colombia. The Commander was a sleek seven-passenger aircraft worth $2 million and prized in the drug trade. It cost another $4 million in duties to bring the aircraft legally into Colombia. To dodge this, drug dealers often bought identical planes and smuggled them out of Florida and into South America. One Commander would be registered legally, while the other — a mirror image of the first — was snuck into the country. This arrangement did not just save duty. It also provided a built-in alibi. If one plane crashed or was seized in a drug bust, its owners could point to the identical twin aircraft and feign innocence about any wrongdoing. How could they be guilty of any crime when their aircraft was in full public view?

Jaworski figured Striedinger was up to some such scam when he agreed to help transport the Commander. Jaworski would fly it out of Florida to St. Martin, near his parents' home in Tortola in the British Virgin Islands. The Colombians would file a flight plan to a nearby island that didn't have an air traffic tower. A few minutes after taking off, the Colombians would call St. Martin to say they had landed, then sneak south to Colombia while Jaworski pocketed $15,000 for a free flight home for Christmas.

One of the high points of the jaunt was when Jaworski was able to make the experienced pilot Striedinger queasy. En route to St. Martin, Jaworski spotted his parents out sailing. "I flew over the boat at about 100 feet," Jaworski later laughed. "Striedinger thought I was going to plow into the water. He was having a heart attack. I was just waving at my parents."

But in January, Jaworski learned the trip was much more serious than he had assumed. The Commander 1000 had been stolen with the help of an airplane dealer named Dave, who had originally sold it to a Colombian named Galiano. Galiano carried considerable clout and a nasty reputation in cartel circles. Before Galiano could take possession of his new plane, Dave the dealer turned it over to Striedinger, then claimed to Galiano that it had been stolen. The dealer told Galiano that he would help him get another plane as soon as Galiano got his insurance money. It was simple and potentially workable, but failed miserably because its plotters totally underestimated the murderous depths of Galiano's ill humor.

Galiano did not want another plane. He did not want to dicker with insurance companies. He wanted the aircraft he had purchased and he wanted it now. And when he found out that he had been tricked, he also wanted revenge.

Galiano's considerable temper was stoked when Dave the airplane dealer glibly told him that if he could not work out something with the insurance company, then Galiano was on his own. Then, sensing that what had seemed to be a simple scam was falling apart at warp speed, Dave nervously sent a middle-aged employee named Fidel Fernandez south to Colombia to smooth things out. Fernandez wasn't told about the theft, so his words would have a ring of innocence when he met Galiano.

Fernandez still wasn't convincing enough. He was strapped to a tree and his arm was snapped. He protested that this was all some terrible mistake, that he knew nothing about the theft. A pin was rammed through his testicles, but failed to jog his memory. His torturers left for three days, and when they returned, Fernandez was still alive and still moaning that he knew nothing about the theft. This time his words had an unmistakable ring of truth and Fernandez was set free.

Shortly after word of Fernandez's fate reached Florida, a man's deep voice was on the telephone line to Dave the airplane dealer, saying, "Dave, your son just put a sticker on the back of his car."

No words could have been more terrifying. "Dave went into shock, because his son was going to university in northern Florida that particular day," Jaworski later recalled. "That kid was putting a parking sticker on his car. Nobody could have known that unless they were there. So Dave freaked. He got on the phone to Roberto and said, 'Bring that goddamn plane right back.' In that particular time, in those three days, Galiano had a private detective up in Gainesville who was tracking Dave's kid. They were watching him. Dave was going wild. I flew up there with his wife and got his kid out of school. It was amazing. I had never seen a guy so scared in my life."

Galiano's fury still hadn't been extinguished. He put a murder contract out on Striedinger and called it off only after Pablo Escobar himself stepped in. Jaworski recalled, "Galiano said to Roberto, 'We're going to let you off this time because of respect for Pablo's wishes. But if you fuck up one more time, you're dead.'"

Amid all this misery and anger, Jaworski spotted a money-making opportunity. He feigned indignation that his associates could stoop so low as to use him in such a scheme, then charged — and received — $25,000 to bring the Commander back to Galiano. But the drama wasn't without a message: run afoul of the cartel and expect to live out your worst nightmare. Even innocent members of your family won't be safe.

This message had special meaning for Jaworski. His Christmas stopover in the Virgin Islands meant Frank the gofer and Roberto Striedinger knew where his parents lived and that he was close to them.

The call came late in the morning, when Jaworski was at the aircraft dealership in Florida. It was from Fruco, a good-time guy and serious drug trafficker. There had been an accident — something about Hans Striedinger and the Jet-Ski. Hans had loved to rev it up to high speed, crouch down, and then shoot under the four-and-a-half-foot helipad.

"I used to think, someday he's going to decapitate himself," Jaworski recalled.

Fruco's voice was shaking. "Doug, Hans has died."

"How the hell did that happen?"

"He was Jet-Skiing and he was trying to do a handstand on the Jet-Ski and he hit the seawall."

Jaworski later recalled, "I spent the next little while trying to figure out how the hell anybody could do a handstand on the Jet-Ski. But it didn't surprise me that he tried it."

It was a couple of months before Jaworski saw Roberto Striedinger again. The father looked drained, desolate, far from his normal, arrogant, controlling self, the legend who could coolly fend off the likes of Pablo Escobar.

Later Jaworski heard that Striedinger's wife, Piedad, blamed the death on the house that once belonged to Nixon. In Piedad's view, Roberto Striedinger was also to blame for buying the mansion and keeping Hans there. Everything would have turned out differently, if not for the old Nixon mansion....

"I was surprised," Jaworski said later. "Piedad had always seemed very reasonable. Everybody could see it coming. I always thought that she was more reasonable than that."

Now the old Nixon mansion was empty, except for Striedinger and people totally under his control, like the servants and call girls supplied by Frank the gofer.

5/ A LETHAL HOBBY

"They were the scum of the earth and proud of it."

— Douglas Jaworski on his associates in the drug cartel.

ALEJANDRO DIEGO VASQUEZ CAYCEDO WAS A man of enormous contradictions. Before he introduced Doug Jaworski to Caycedo, Frank the gofer said that Caycedo was "really big," and in Frank's world view, bigness meant closeness to drug baron Pablo Escobar. Yet there was Caycedo in a Medellin apartment, tenderly cradling a relative's newborn baby, while conducting a drug deal on a portable phone. The scene was simultaneously callous and tender. Handsome, well spoken, and in his mid-thirties, Caycedo kept eight apartments, more for security than for his innumerable mistresses. Since he added and dropped an apartment a month, authorities and underworld enemies never quite knew his exact location. But the furniture — including a rich assortment of soft leather couches — remained the same, giving the arrangement an odd feeling of permanence and hominess.

The day that Jaworski met Caycedo for the first time, in the spring of 1988, a half dozen bodyguards sat transfixed in front of a television, watching a well-worn pornographic video, their eyes glazed and their .38 revolvers at arm's reach.

For Caycedo's underlings, the apartments were places to crash when they were in the city or to sneak girlfriends into if they were cheating on their wives. And if they woke up at a reasonable hour in the morning, the same maid who changed the bed sheets and towels would serve them scrambled eggs, ham, and distinctive Colombian cheese, coffee, and pan-fried bread.

By getting into the apartment and meeting Caycedo, Jaworski already knew more about the cocaine multimillionaire than any police officer in Canada. Canadian police intelligence authorities didn't even know that Caycedo existed, let alone that he planned to ship billions of dollars of the addictive white powder through Canada and into the rich American market.

Caycedo's boss, Pablo Escobar, was known wherever police fought the cocaine trade. Escobar was the chief suspect in innumerable murders, ranging from that of crusading Colombian Justice Minister Rodrigo Lara-Bonilla to those of religious workers and street vendors. Escobar's reputation was so grisly — even by cartel standards — that Caycedo would instruct his pilots that, if they were captured by authorities, they should blame everything on Escobar. Escobar didn't mind. "Escobar had so much against him that it didn't matter," Jaworski explained. "After you've been blamed for 100 murders, being blamed for 101 doesn't matter."

The day that Jaworski first met Caycedo, the Colombian wanted to talk about planes — Commander 980s in particular. The Commanders were perfect drug planes: strong, fast, capable of carrying a huge payload, and rugged enough for jungle landings. Caycedo wanted to buy one from Jaworski for $600,000 (U.S.). The price would soon shoot to $750,000

(U.S.), then close to $1 million (U.S.). Since production had halted on the 980s, they were in increasingly short supply and drug runners raced to buy up the remaining ones.

Jaworski was no innocent about the underworld, but there was plenty left to learn. Frank the gofer told him on this first trip to meet Caycedo that the cartel planned to fly in bundles of low-currency bills from Japan, Germany, and the United States. The money would be bleached white, then reprinted with higher denominations, since duplicating paper is the toughest part of a counterfeiter's art. Jaworski found it interesting that each day one of the bodyguards was dispatched to collect faxes and deliver them to Caycedo. The faxes included confidential court records from drug trials, aircraft specifications, and newspaper coverage of drug seizures and trials. Cartel lawyers were clearly expected to do much more than argue fine points of the law in an orderly fashion. While Caycedo was physically far from the major markets of North America, he was not in the dark about them. Colombia might suffer from soul-destroying poverty and Third World education, sanitation, hospitals, and food for the majority of its people, but it had a state-of-the-art paging system that flashed alphanumeric messages across the portable screens of drug barons. Such high-tech devices let Caycedo invade and flee North America simultaneously, without ever leaving Colombia. The costs included a $40,000 monthly phone bill, but the far-reaching control offered by the long-distance lines was more than worth the expense.

Two months after that first meeting with Caycedo, Jaworski got a phone call in Fort Lauderdale.

"My brother's going to call you up and he'll pay you for the plane," Caycedo said.

The next day, Caycedo's younger brother, Fausto, presented Jaworski with a brown paper bag containing a $60,000 (U.S.) deposit for the Commander.

When he delivered the plane, Jaworski found a major mood shift in Caycedo. Jaworski had not cheated him. He was a rare commodity.

Caycedo was now cheerful and expansive, as they sat on the downstairs pink couch in his best safehouse in Medellin. Caycedo pulled out maps and began talking of new drug-smuggling routes he was considering. Jaworski took out aircraft listings and showed what was available for Caycedo to buy, with a 10 percent commission to Jaworski.

Association with the likes of Caycedo meant the promise of many more bags of money. But Jaworski had grown up well off and took comfort for granted. For him, Caycedo meant something much more addictive than money or cocaine. In his twenty-six years, Jaworski had never seen anyone like Caycedo. Colombia's ruling classes have a history of enjoying intellectual conversation, and even a drug baron like Caycedo was not shy about discussing life and crime. Indeed, for Caycedo, the two were often synonymous. As they chatted on Caycedo's leather couches, Jaworski felt he was peering into an intriguing, upside-down kingdom. It wasn't really centered on cocaine, but on breaking the law. "The thing I found fascinating about Caycedo was his view on life. It was so different. It was a perspective from the cartel side of things. They have a whole other way of looking at everything. I don't think he had any particular fascination for dope. I don't think he cared what it was. It could have been coffee beans. The underlings would talk about somebody and say, he is a big guy. But a big guy means that he's a bigger crook than you are. You're supposed to honor the guy because he's a bigger crook than the other crooks. The lower you go, apparently, the bigger you get.

"But the underworld and the overworld have tremendous connections. They all have to do with two things: business and law. It's not just a bunch of dirtbags living off this. If they made this legal all of a sudden, there would be a helluva lot of cops out of work. There would be a helluva lot of lawyers out of work, too."

It was an interesting theory and a comforting one for those who made their living exporting misery. To them, average, law-abiding people were hypocrites, while the criminals were honest, since they freely admitted their corruption. Once one could believe this, the rest of cartel life came easily and without guilt.

Jaworski noted paradoxes in Caycedo's world. Here was a multimillionaire who would argue over petty amounts of cash, a soft-spoken man who was never gratuitously violent around Jaworski, yet who surrounded himself with killers. He had a magnificent collection of artwork, and a solid gold pre-Columbian mask encased in Plexiglass. But the artifact was left lying on the floor of Caycedo's condominium apartment as if it didn't matter. Caycedo also gave prominent wall space to a zebra skin and stuffed cattle heads, a reminder of his sprawling 35,000-acre ranch straddling the Venezuelan border in remote west-central Colombia.

The mobsters Doug Jaworski met in Colombia were far different from the Hollywood depictions of old Italian mafiosi. Hollywood's Mafia dons savored respect, tradition, and finesse. Such men — and Mafia leaders were invariably men — loved to do someone a favor today to gain an ally for future struggles. Elders were treated with dignity, and the most skillful ones died peacefully in bed. Drug trafficking was viewed with disdain and was only one of many criminal activities practiced.

But the members of the real-life Medellin cartel were young, immature, and brutal, and the cartel existed solely to traffic cocaine. They often referred to themselves as "the Mafia," but unlike their Italian counterpart, they had no blood initiations, solemn oaths, or mythology about respect and respectability. The cartel was born in 1981, after leftist guerrillas kidnapped a relative of a major trafficker, and competition among 200 Colombian organizations, and rival Cubans, created a sea of blood in Florida. The cartels' members were far more pragmatic and violent than the fictitious Corleone family of the *Godfather* movies. Jaworski recalled, "They wouldn't go around kissing each other's hands (like the Mafia). There's none of that crap. In that business, your life span is so short that, if you're going to be big, you're not going to be big for long. Accounts are settled daily in the coke business. You don't owe somebody favors. You don't do anything for free."

And unlike the Hollywood villains who wore superbly cut Armani suits to commit their crimes, in the real world of organized crime that Jaworski knew, even multimillionaires seldom wore anything but designer jeans, polo shirts, and leather jackets. Rolex watches were popular too, although Caycedo favored a wafer-thin, gold designer timepiece. As a slight affectation, Caycedo had his jeans flown down from the United States, preferring the feel of imported Calvin Kleins and Levis to locally available brands. And while cartel barons might wear belts and loafers with the Gucci label, they were often the cheaper rip-off items, made in Venezuela. "Not everybody loses their sense of what's reasonable to pay for clothes. I never saw anybody in a suit," Jaworski said.

During his visits to Colombia, Jaworski found Caycedo's love life a source of amusement. Despite his avoirdupois and a jutting chin like that of Canadian prime minister Brian Mulroney, the drug baron was a good-looking man who was constantly falling in love with breathtakingly beautiful women. Invariably, they were frightened off by his common-law wife, a woman whose criminal reputation was as formidable as her jewelry collection. "They would get freaked out when they found out who his wife was, and they wouldn't go out with him any more because they were always afraid that his wife would kill them. She wasn't very good-looking, but she had a very authoritative effect. She had a lot of jewelry — beautiful jewelry, diamonds and sapphires. It was amazing."

Most of the women who passed through Caycedo's life and bedrooms were brought in by a small man in his fifties named Alex. He wasn't much to look at and walked with a limp, but when he arrived at the safehouses, it was invariably with a selection of stunning beauties. Sometimes, Caycedo himself went out on the prowl, but this had to be done with caution and discretion, because of the dangers of his work. "Caycedo wouldn't go cruising the bars," Jaworski said. "He'd go to a discotheque, but only ones that were organizationally owned. There were good-looking girls there, but you had to be careful you didn't stomp on somebody else's territory."

Jaworski found that Caycedo knew how to play host. "He used to keep me in one of his apartments. It's funny working with Caycedo. At about eight o'clock, business stops and these girls show up. I don't know where the hell they come from, but he gets about five or six of the most beautiful women in the world. They show up, out comes the liquor, and everybody has a little party right there. They shoot the shit and talk and screw and everything else. Everybody drinks whisky there. It's a cowboy drink, I guess."

Even during his parties, Caycedo never used cocaine. He didn't even speak the drug's name, preferring to call it "merchandise." There was enough adrenalin from his work that he didn't need the chemically induced kind. Caycedo's attitude toward his product was disdainful, Jaworski found. "He never felt guilty. It's the only way you can make money down there. It was like, 'Wake up and smell the coffee.' That's the way it is. He never used the stuff himself. He thought that people who did use it were low-lifes; that if you want to put that shit up your nose, that's fine."

And there were enough real things for Caycedo to guard

against, without the crippling paranoia that consumption of the white powder often brings. Most cartel barons had learned their lesson about consuming cocaine from the bloody drug wars of the 1960s, when Colombians shoved their way into the North American drug market. First, they were suppliers to the Cuban cocaine dealers who moved to south Florida after Fidel Castro came to power. The Cubans were eventually and brutally pushed aside. Then the Colombian newcomers began fighting viciously among themselves for territory in North America. Self-destructive vendettas — often fueled by the paranoia of overindulgence in cocaine — were slowing business. The second generation of Colombian cocaine traffickers were also jittery about the kidnappings that their new-found wealth had attracted. Despite his omnipresent bodyguards, Caycedo invariably also wore a .38 revolver, to the point that Jaworski speculated it left a permanent indentation in Caycedo's slightly paunchy waist.

Jaworski knew he was in the company of gangsters, but he didn't particularly care. The money was great, the company perversely unique, and Jaworski could rationalize his association with Caycedo by saying that he was only selling planes, and that if he didn't sell them to the cocaine cartel, someone else would.

"I enjoyed working with Diego because he presented a view of life that I could never even imagine myself. I liked him because he was so interesting. They're the scumbags of the world and they're proud of it.

"He used to describe the drug dealing as his hobby. He loved doing it. He loved the action and the pace and the power that he got from having thirty bodyguards. These guys would come out of the woodwork, young guys with .38s. Wherever Diego would go, there had to be a car in front and a car behind and they all had radios so that they could talk to each other. If there was an army roadblock and the guards in the first car saw they were going to be stopped, they'd radio back and tell Diego to go another route.

"You might ask why he didn't quit after he made his first $20 million. Go back to square one, pal. It's his hobby. It's the power thing. He's like a little dictator. Those bodyguards don't move without asking him.

"But he still thinks he's going to retire and buy an island somewhere and live on it. He was always going to retire next month. A couple more big deals and he'd retire."

Many of the cocaine networks were formed back in the 1960s when they transported marijuana, a drug that once had symbolized peace, nonviolence, and sharing. Now, the networks had crystallized into a corporate structure committed to unbridled, bloody free enterprise. One of Colombia's young cocaine lords, Carlos Enrique Lehder, had tried to put a socio-political slant on his crime, arguing in a strange mélange of hippie philosophy and neo-Nazism that the cocaine trade was the Third World's revenge for Yankee imperialism.

During his frequent chats with Jaworski, Caycedo never bothered to put his drug dealing into such grand political terms. If he had, it was doubtful Jaworski would have believed it. But during their frequent chats in Caycedo's safehouses, the drug baron expressed some political views too, such as an absolute revulsion for left-wing guerrillas, even though they sometimes made useful hit men. Some day, the army would lose its battle against the guerrillas, and then it would be up to the cartel to suppress them, Caycedo told Jaworski.

"These guys don't seem to have a God," Jaworski said. "Their God is money. That's all they care about. I can't say if that's because they grew up so poor. But it's a fact, not an opinion, that their God is money and that's all they give a shit about."

Caycedo and the Medellin drug barons generated their wealth from a center that has been called the city of eternal spring. Medellin was beautiful from a distance, but Jaworski noted, "When you get down and see the slums — the open sewers, the rotten housing — it just makes you disbelieve that people can live like that." People were moving to Medellin from the surrounding mountains in hopes of finding work. The life they found in the slums was a marked contrast to the life Jaworski had known.

"I certainly did see some rich people in Medellin and I saw absolute poverty in Medellin, too. It's not like here in Canada. It's a class society down there. There are people who have money and there are people who don't have money and that's it in Medellin.

"And the people who do have money make sure that every person who doesn't have money knows it. Just by the way that their dialect is, the way that they speak. In restaurants, they speak down to waiters and waitresses. Taxi drivers are scumbags. They snap at them and they're not polite to them. This is done by people who have money and have never earned it and don't really know how to spend it.

"But I was always friendly with taxi drivers and waiters. I used to joke with Caycedo's elderly maid. I'm probably the only person who ever paid any attention to her. On one trip, she asked me if I could bring her a Rolex watch the next time I came. I asked her if she wanted a fake one or a real one. She said a real one. She was serious. But I can't blame her for trying. I thought, 'Whoa. Maybe I'm paying too much attention to her.' I like to think that every person I come across in my life will remember me."

Jaworski could fit in with Caycedo because, while he might like to joke with waiters and maids, he did not spend time worrying about the poor and how their lot might be improved.

He later said, "There have always been poor people in Colombia. I don't know who's responsible. I have no idea. For some unknown reason, I guess there have to be poor people."

Power in Colombia has a personal, elitist flavor. The state never really caught hold after the old Spanish rulers were forced out by warlords. The country suffered through eight civil wars in the nineteenth century and an agonizing and protracted upheaval known as "La Violencia" in the mid-twentieth century, which brought 200,000 deaths. Caycedo seemed more than comfortable with his role in this tradition. He gave the impression of having been born to higher classes than his bodyguards. Although he didn't talk much about his past, he appeared educated and Jaworski heard that he had spent about a decade in Los Angeles before moving back to Medellin.

Caycedo had a dismissive attitude toward state power, both abroad and at home. There were still dangers and irritations, like a general who had the nerve to throw Caycedo in jail for three days for having a suspicious map. The general proved to be a difficult target for cartel hit squads, but Caycedo generally took such setbacks in stride.

One night, Jaworski heard pops from outside one of Caycedo's Medellin apartments.

"Come here. Come here. Come over to the window," Jaworski said.

"Yeah?" Caycedo said, walking over from the television, which he generally tuned to the CNN all-news network.

"Is that a machine gun or what?" Jaworski asked.

"Might be, or might just be fireworks," Caycedo replied casually, then walked back to the television.

They never learned who was being shot at, if indeed it was machine-gun fire. To Caycedo, it wasn't particularly important since it wasn't directed at him. Jaworski recalled, "Diego used to say that the only way they'd stop the drug traffic was to make it legal. Take the crime out of it. He figures that they'll do it someday, but until that day, he's got himself a great business."

Caycedo wasn't always so blasé. During one trip, Caycedo and Jaworski had a couple of hours to kill before Jaworski flew back to Florida. Jaworski had just dropped off another Commander and was together with Caycedo and a bodyguard in one car, accompanied by another car full of guards. They backed into spaces at a cantina parking lot, as they always did. That way, they wouldn't have to slam them into reverse for a quick getaway.

Normally, Caycedo stayed home and ordered out from one of the city's best restaurants. But they were hungry and the little husband-and-wife cantina with just a dozen tables looked safe. Caycedo gave the impression that he had been there before and that it was secure. The menu that was printed on the place mats was cheap and basic: chicken and rice, meat and potatoes. That was in keeping with the decor: white paint on concrete walls, ceiling fans, and crude, handmade wooden furniture that was constructed with an eye toward low costs, not quality craftsmanship.

The bodyguards sat at a nearby table, sipping Cokes, while surveying the street and other tables. As usual, Caycedo wore his .38 on his belt. The situation seemed under control.

"I can't even go to a restaurant," Caycedo said. He was clearly upset.

"What do you mean?" Jaworski asked.

"Look at the bodyguards," Caycedo said, gesturing toward their table.

"Do you think other people in here know — ?" Jaworski said. He didn't have to complete the sentence and say, "know you're a top drug dealer."

"They know. They all know." Caycedo wasn't embarrassed. Just disgusted.

6/ THE ANGRY GOFER

"I'm going to get you someday."

— Douglas Jaworski makes an enemy in the cartel.

"I KNOW YOU'RE GOING TO SCREW ME eventually," Frank the gofer would constantly tell Jaworski.

Striedinger's gofer expected to be paid half of everything Jaworski made from selling and servicing planes for Caycedo. He believed this was his due, since he had introduced Jaworski to the cartel baron.

"No, I'm not," Jaworski would reply. Perhaps Frank the gofer sensed a rich-boy sneer as Jaworski continued, "Frank. Buddy."

But Frank the gofer wasn't a total simpleton. He knew they were never really buddies. Like Jaworski, Frank the gofer was a hustler. But he was well into his fifties and still lived hand to mouth, scam to scam. His boss, Roberto Striedinger, had mansions in two countries. Frank the gofer wasn't poor, but he had to scrape to pay the mortgage on his townhouse.

Striedinger didn't pay him a salary. Frank the gofer had to constantly hatch schemes of his own or ask Striedinger for money. It was a good way of reminding him who was in control.

To make ends meet, Frank the gofer could always do a little drug selling. He functioned one level above street pushers, providing a link between sellers who wanted drugs and those with a little to spare. For his services as an intermediary, he would make about $1,000 on a $20,000 deal. Frank the gofer dealt in single-kilo amounts, while Caycedo wouldn't waste his breath on anything less than a 100-kilo transaction.

Frank the gofer lived in the shadow of millionaires and was used to doing things on a modest scale. He still clung to dreams, however. He believed that his future was in aviation and that some day he would sell airplanes big time, even though he couldn't fix them or fly well. He had plans to have his picture taken with every plane he sold, even though he didn't own a camera.

Striedinger wore silks and linens, in subtle shades of tan, cream, and brown, offset by top-of-the-line Bally shoes. Frank the gofer was invariably decked out more modestly, in well-worn jeans, a white T-shirt, and imitation Adidas. To hear Frank the gofer describe things, Striedinger was a veritable bionic man in the bedroom. One of Frank the gofer's varied chores was to line up women for him. Frank the gofer was overwhelmed by his employer's demands. He told Jaworski that Striedinger could apparently service a parade of four women half his age in just one afternoon in the old Nixon mansion.

"I don't know what he does with them," Frank the gofer said in wonder. "I can't figure out what he does with them."

Jaworski thought about it and started to wonder, too.

For Frank the gofer, there was his often-cranky wife and flings in Medellin with a clerk from a clothing boutique at the

Las Vegas Mall there. His mistress was short and a little pudgy and generally homely. But Frank himself was no Kevin Costner and found her a comfortable companion. She seemed attracted to him, or more particularly to his promises that some day soon he would bring her to Miami.

A few months after the Commander debacle involving Galiano, Jaworski and Frank the gofer were in the air together again. This time, they were flying an eight-passenger Queen-Air twin-engine plane to Colombia. The engines and fuel tanks were modified to allow it to fly extra distances and a rear door that opened inward had been created. That made it easier to make high-speed cocaine drops into the water, something popular in the mid-1980s.

The plane had been rented out by its owner to drug dealers. This was a common arrangement. Even Caycedo found it prohibitive to keep a full fleet of aircraft in the air. Kiko Mencada of Medellin owned between thirty and thirty-five aircraft and would rent them to men like Caycedo for $1 million a flight, which is roughly the value of the planes, before taxes. For this, renters got a fully maintained aircraft. If it crashed, Kiko would have to eat the loss, something made easier by his extensive real estate holdings.

For the trip, Frank the gofer had a little bag and a cooler. While over Haiti, Jaworski turned to him and asked, "What's in the cooler?"

"Oh, I don't think you want to eat what's in the cooler," he replied. "There're frogs in there."

"Liar!" Jaworski laughed and popped open the lid, expecting a sandwich and a Coke.

With that, a green frog leapt out and began hopping about the plane. The frog was pioneer breeding stock for what Frank the gofer hoped would someday be a gourmet frog ranch. He had read all about frog farming in a magazine and now he planned to make his mark by setting up a little operation on the 100,000-acre cattle ranch Striedinger owned outside Bogota.

Striedinger had shown that big money could be made from producing food delicacies, with his shrimp farm and the factory where hearts of palm were packaged as specialty food. Shipping tinned goods was also a natural cover for smuggling. Frank the gofer's nine pioneering frogs were to be his entree into the same line of business.

Frank the gofer had once also tried copying Striedinger's shrimp business on a smaller scale. He had proudly passed about shiny gold business cards with his name alongside a picture of a shrimp, listing his business as "Acuaculture equipment and supplies." Somehow, he failed to impress any potential investors.

Now, with the frog venture, Frank the gofer busied himself setting up little fences in a stream running through Striedinger's cattle ranch. There, he hoped, his breeding stock of nine American frogs would multiply, as would the profits. Once again, it was a humiliating defeat, Jaworski later laughed. "The whole project just sort of flopped, like everything else in his life."

During one visit to Fort Lauderdale, Frank the gofer bought a single-engine Cessna 206, then had extra fuel tanks added on to allow it to fly to Colombia from Florida nonstop. Once the work was done, Frank the gofer offered Jaworski $1,000, plus expenses, to fly the Cessna to Colombia. Jaworski never balked at easy, quick money or adventure and didn't back out when, at the last minute, the destination was switched to the Bahamas. Once there, Jaworski was finally told the true purpose of the flight; they were going to bust out of jail three Colombian pilots who had been caught trafficking cocaine. "I didn't like to see these guys in jail so it wasn't any personal problem for me," Jaworski later said.

A Nassau lawyer who had been bribed $300,000 for his role

in the breakout had doctored a release order for a client who was behind bars for being vagrant and drunk. The drug traffickers' names were typed onto the release order, which was handed to a jail guard. Even if the guard looked carefully at the release order, it didn't matter. He had also been paid off.

Such capers were routine for the cartel in the Bahamas in the mid–1980s. The Caribbean had become a cocaine sea after Colombian cartel boss Carlos Lehder bought land in the Bahamas and used the island as a strategic transit point for American-bound drugs. Government probes found that police officials had sometimes helped traffickers unload and guard drug shipments. Corruption went even higher as three Bahamian cabinet ministers resigned and two were fired after a 1984 commission of inquiry into the drug trade's impact on the islands. The crooked lawyer had once been a prosecutor for the government while a dishonest senior Bahamian immigration official oversaw the escape to see it proceeded smoothly.

The whole jail-break idea was hilarious to Jaworski. He flew the Colombians down to an abandoned airstrip at Rock Sound. He planned to get off in the Bahamas, then return home on a commercial flight while the escaped prisoners flew off to Colombia. The jail break went without a hitch, but in the fugitives' hurry and the joy of the escape, they took off before Jaworski could get the bag holding his passport out of the departing Cessna.

He tried to get past the officials without it, but an island police officer thought he looked suspicious as he stood in line to buy a ticket. The joke was now over, as Jaworski found himself confined to a tiny police station that stank of urine.

That night, the crooked attorney behind the phony release bond showed up.

"You get me out of here or I'm going to tell these guys what you did," Jaworski said.

The threat worked. The next morning, the island police were $10,000 richer, and Jaworski was free again. Five days after that, his passport arrived in the mail from the fugitive pilots, who were so grateful that they were willing to forgo the couple of thousand dollars they could make doctoring and reselling it.

Frank the gofer seemed reasonably content with his lot. He always had his plans and hopes of the big break that would put him in charge of his own destiny. But when he showed up at Jaworski's aircraft shop in the spring of 1988, he was livid.

"You fucked me, you motherfucker!" he screamed at Jaworski. "Hit me! Come on. Hit me!" It was gut-rot, undiluted anger. Desperate, pathetic frustration and hurt.

Frank the gofer clearly wanted a brawl, but couldn't bring himself to land the first punch. He gave the impression he would go wild, if only Jaworski would throw the first punch and free him.

The staff at the airplane dealership stared at the spectacle on the ramp. They all knew Frank the gofer.

"Everybody was watching him like he was a nut," Jaworski recalled. "They all knew who he was but none of them respected him. He had been trying to get a private pilot's license for more than six months. I felt sort of sorry for him, but I wanted him to get away from the employees. It just wasn't the place for that sort of thing."

The reason Frank the gofer was furious was that he had learned that Jaworski and Caycedo were negotiating aircraft sales and he had been cut out. Jaworski said later that Frank the gofer simply had no skills to offer and couldn't go on expecting a percentage for nothing. And yet he genuinely seemed to believe that he had been cheated.

"He knew it was coming but when the reality sank in, he went nuts," Jaworski said.

Frank the gofer made a promise before he turned on his heels and walked away.

"I'm going to fuck you some day," he shouted. "But I'm not going to go to the police to do it. One thing I will never do is go to the police. But I will get you some day."

Frank the gofer couldn't get respect. He couldn't get the money that he thought he deserved. He couldn't even get a punch in the face. But now he could dream of revenge and soon he would get his chance.

7/ THE HOME FRONT

"She hated it."

— Douglas Jaworski's honeymoon ends abruptly.

SUSAN LOOKED UNATTAINABLE TO JAWORSKI and maybe that was part of the attraction. She lived in the same apartment complex in Fort Lauderdale as he did, and everything about her was impressive to the young man in his early twenties, now making his way in the aircraft business. Four years older than Jaworski, Susan was blessed with blonde, blue-eyed Scandinavian beauty and a quick mind that enabled her to earn three college degrees and a yearly salary of close to $100,000. She had even once completed a marathon. "I remember being interested in her and she wouldn't even give me the time of day," Jaworski later said. "I thought she was out of reach, older, better looking, smarter. I always thought Susan was the most intelligent woman I ever met."

One night, some mutual friends invited them both for a night on the town and, to Jaworski's surprise, she seemed attracted to something about him. They started dating and after four years moved in together. Susan enjoyed the wealth Doug's unsavory connections brought. They dined out frequently, called a cleaning service when their apartment was messy, and took frequent outings on Doug's boats and planes.

Susan and Doug often went to parties where cocaine was a designer drug for the young and the wealthy. It was everywhere in their world then, although they abstained from its use. Young professionals who would never consider injecting themselves with heroin like some low-grade junkie found that snorting cocaine had a certain cachet. Jaworski laughed when he remembered the party at which a judge, doctor, and police officer jokingly toasted through their noses, all smiling ironically as they said, "To crime."

Six months after they moved in together, Doug and Susan were engaged. Susan planned their wedding. It was to be held on a beach at sunset with a live calypso band playing on. But Doug wanted to handle the honeymoon himself and he wanted it to be a surprise. The only hint he gave her was to tell her to get shots for tropical diseases. Because of the needles, she was violently ill the night before her wedding.

Susan had twelve days off work and wanted sun and relaxation for their honeymoon. She smiled when Doug showed her a pair of tickets to Paris, then Rome, and told her to dress casually. Susan packed silks and cheerfully climbed aboard the jetliner.

On arrival at the Paris airport, he turned to her and said, "Have fun shopping and do all the sightseeing you can. But we have got to catch another plane in two hours."

"Okay," Susan replied, still happy. "We're going to Rome."

On the approach to Rome, he said, "Better take a quick look at the Colosseum because we've got another flight to catch."

This time it was only a one-hour stopover. Again, they did not get out of the airport, and Susan was no longer smiling.

The next plane they boarded was destined for the Ivory Coast.

"We're not going to pick up that plane, are we?" Susan asked. She was referring to an aircraft belonging to Florida aircraft dealer Fidel Fernandez. He was the same man who had been strapped to the tree and tortured by Galiano. Now, in a dramatic example of how allegiances can shift in the drug trade, he and Galiano were conducting millions of dollars of aircraft business together.

Unfortunately for Susan, her guess was right. They were going to use their honeymoon to pick up the plane.

"I just deflated," Jaworski later recalled. He had thought she would love the adventure and could not have been more wrong. He later said, "Lots of ferry pilots fly the North Atlantic routes, which I had done many times. But the South Atlantic routes; there're not too many guys who have done that." Susan was still not impressed.

"She hated it. It was a complete mystery to her. She didn't particularly feel comfortable in a little airplane and, after all the pressures of getting married and the pressures of organizing a wedding, she wanted to go and relax on a beach in Hawaii in the sun."

She also wanted to get back to work in twelve days, not hop-step across Africa before heading off on a little-traveled thirteen-hour South Atlantic crossing. "That wasn't for me," Jaworski said of a Hawaiian beach honeymoon. "I wanted something exciting."

So Susan spent the next seven days inside the small plane, where she was given the task of holding a flashlight as Doug changed fuel tanks. A minute before a tank was to run empty, he turned to Susan and said, "Give me the light."

"I can't find the light."

It was pitch black, except for lightning flashing in the distance. They were somewhere between Abidjan in the Ivory Coast and Dakar, Senegal. The plane had two engines and, in a few seconds, one would be out of gas. It was already sputtering.

"Susan, get the light!"

In aircraft, problems come in groups of ten. If they are not solved adequately and quickly, they culminate in crashes.

"Susan, get the fucking light!"

Now Susan was sobbing. "Oh, we're going to die! We're going to die!"

Jaworski was starting to panic. He was losing control of the situation. Susan was too distraught to look for the light any more. Jaworski groped for a valve in the dark and found it. With a flip of a switch, the engine was back to life. Susan kept on sobbing, but then people are often harder to control than machinery.

"We could have really enjoyed that trip back," Jaworski said later. "There was no timetable as far as I was concerned. But she had to be back in twelve days to go back to work. We had to race through that trip, which made it completely uncomfortable, just so that she could get back to work. And there was no amount of begging and pleading that I could do to get her to change her mind. This was the first indication of how committed she was to her work."

Once the honeymoon trip was over, Jaworski asked her, "Would you do it all over again?"

"Yes," Susan replied. "But next time with a little more notice."

"She used to brag about it all the time," Jaworski said.

Within a year, that honeymoon flight would seem like one of the more relaxing events of their marriage.

8/ BETRAYAL

"Help, the paranoids are after me."

— Douglas Jaworski's joke.

JAWORSKI'S OLD FRIEND WAS NERVOUS AND wanted to talk. Things had started to go really well in his home life, the friend said, but his business world was exploding. A secretary at a law office that had set up the friend's money-laundering corporation was talking to police. Now police as well as the IRS were investigating Jaworski's friend for money-laundering and for drug trafficking. He was no master criminal but he had broken the law, and they were bound to find something. His ventures included setting up a marijuana patch in Iowa, but that had gone badly. Deer wandered into the field, sampled some of the harvest, then trampled the rest.

The IRS had the reputation of grabbing cases like a wolverine on a doe's back. Could Jaworski help? More specifically, could he lend his friend $25,000 to hire a lawyer?

"He knew he had fucked up bad," Jaworski recalled later.

"He told me that there was a potentially disastrous situation for him coming up in Minnesota where he was sending dope to guys through Air Express. Apparently the guy he was sending it to got caught and his name and address were on the return packet."

On the flip side of the plea for help was a threat: either come up with the $25,000 or get implicated for any number of crimes. The last thing Jaworski needed was the authorities poking into his new wealth. Jaworski later explained that he modeled his network of offshore corporations on the tanker ship industry. "Texaco isn't going to borrow from an American bank to purchase a ship that's going to carry oil. That's ridiculous. They borrow money from Switzerland, which has cheaper interest rates, to buy a ship that transports oil and is registered in Liberia or Panama. That way you don't have to deal with the Coast Guard regulations for the upkeep of the ship, and the interest and the taxes are cheaper."

Even before he talked to his friend, Jaworski knew something was wrong. His bank records in Broward County had been subpoenaed in the spring of 1988. He had hired two lawyers, but they ran up against a stone wall. Now his friend was making things worse. Jaworski might even get nabbed for a crime he did not commit.

When you hang around serious criminals, certain things are basic truths, like the fact that the people who are closest to you are the ones who can cause the most damage. Or that little details and seemingly ordinary people — like chatty secretaries in law firms — can quickly be molded into the bullets that can kill you. That paranoia, not guilt, causes many criminals to self-destruct and drag others with them. And that paranoia is also a totally appropriate response to some situations. How could Jaworski not worry, especially considering what he had heard about police holding cells and prison? There's a joke that, if you're young, boyish, and soft like Jaworski, you had better learn to dance or box if you're sent to prison. Jaworski had grown up accustomed to privilege and freedom and was no fighter. The prospect of being raped in a cell disgusted him. Even if he was safe from other prisoners, the thought of life behind bars was unimaginable. One week of working in a Toronto darkroom when he was sixteen had been too much for him.

A chameleon needs air, not enclosure, possibilities, not confinement. It can look threatening to those who don't know it well. But its bite isn't much to fear. Its real strength is its adaptability.

Sure, he'd help out with the $25,000, Jaworski told his old friend.

Then he started to worry some more. After all, the lawyers were going to protect his friend, not him. Something had to change.

Back in Colombia, Caycedo was making a pest of himself. Jaworski had brought some tarps to his farm during one of his visits. Caycedo called from 400 miles away in Medellin to ask how many tarps there were. A worker hopped on a motorcycle, rode three miles to the plane, opened the tarp packages and counted them, then rode back and radioed the news to Caycedo. "What size are these new tarps?" Caycedo asked. That meant another trip out to the plane; another report to Caycedo. "By the way, what color were they?" Caycedo now asked. All the details were invariably written in tiny handwriting into the reporter's notebooks Caycedo always carried.

"It used to just make those guys nuts," Jaworski recalled. "Every time they'd get the answer and they'd go back and radio it to him, he'd come back with another request about it."

It was the same way when a couple of cases of Coca-Cola or bags of potatoes were brought out to the farm, or when

Jaworski arrived with a cargo of Reebok and Nike running shoes for the bodyguards. Jaworski enjoyed going to a Foot Locker store at a local Fort Lauderdale mall and loading up with fifteen or so pairs of fashion sneakers in the latest fancy designs. He didn't bother to check exact sizes. It was more fun to watch the bodyguards scramble for the good ones, the sneakers that allowed them to make their own personal fashion statements. The cost of the shoes was factored into Caycedo's bill and everyone was happy.

"All the bodyguards loved to get American running shoes," Jaworski said. "American everything, but running shoes in particular. They always thought that American things had better quality. It was always nice for them to say, 'Oh, I got these in Miami.' They talk bad about the United States but they all want to go there."

The men that Caycedo nagged for petty details about tarps or potatoes or sneakers might be killers several times over. But they always had to be polite to Caycedo, calling him sir. Caycedo was someone big, someone close to Pablo Escobar.

It wasn't that Caycedo didn't have bigger things to worry about. It was just that he knew only too well the direct relationship between tiny details and disasters. If Caycedo had worked for a legitimate business, he would have had a title like senior vice-president in charge of air transportation. Other millionaires with equal power in the cartel handled smuggling cocaine in merchant marine vessels, manufacturing, enforcement, corruption of officials, and other aspects of the cartel's business, much as General Motors has senior managers specializing in things such as styling, marketing, and labor relations. By the late 1980s, when Jaworski arrived on the scene in Colombia, Caycedo's branch of the cartel faced a challenge.

Popular attitudes toward cocaine were becoming more negative. An American agent, Enrique (Kiki) Camarana, had been murdered by drug traffickers in Mexico and low-cost crack cocaine was inflaming street violence in American ghettos. There were now regular and horrific stories of babies being born addicted to the drug. Crack makes a person temporarily feel superhuman, then the paranoia sets in. Heroin users eventually shrivel up, becoming pathetic and passive. But crack addicts tend to go down in a blaze of glory. Soon, the ugliness was spreading north to Canadian neighborhoods as well.

With the shift in public opinion, surveillance for cocaine smuggling had intensified across the southern shoreline of the United States, including Florida. Mexico remained an old standby as an alternative route. But ironically the police and army there were sometimes too corrupt for even the cartel's tastes, cheating both their government and the cocaine barons. In January 1987, the new governor of the Mexican region of Sinaloa fired 1,300 state police officers and ordered roughly 100 prosecuted for corruption. Some 700 members of the Mexican Federal Judicial Police and Federal Security Directorate were also fired, and the directors of both organizations were replaced after the furor over Camarana's 1985 murder. The cartel can still make a hefty profit even if it loses half its drug shipments, so Caycedo kept moving cocaine through Mexico, but expenses there were considered too high. As Jaworski said, "He always asked me if I wanted to fly to Mexico. He wouldn't spell out why. He didn't need to. He wasn't coy about it at all. It was all very open. He talked about it. His job was simply to think of ways to smuggle dope. So he asked me to fly to Mexico. But they could never rely on the Mexican army not to fuck them. They paid off the Mexican army but they were unreliable. It seemed like the Mexican army would accept these payments until they started getting heat from their boss, and then they'd bust these guys. Then they'd say, 'We don't know what happened. We're sorry.'"

Jaworski had no moral objections to moving drugs. He was just afraid of the considerable risks. In his early twenties, before he met Caycedo, he had been involved in a conspiracy to smuggle 240 kilos of cocaine. Jaworski sold boats and aircraft to drug smugglers with Bolivian ties and lined up manpower to move the drugs. Recruited to help out was Michael Little, a former Libertarian Party member and Air Canada pilot who was then flying for a small British Columbia company. Michael Little would eventually move to Bolivia, where he lived with a prostitute and became hooked on crack cocaine. He surfaced again in Miami, helping the Drug Enforcement Administration gain some arrests before Pablo Escobar apparently learned of his duplicity and refused to work with him. Little moved back to Bolivia, where his life ended on a street corner in a hail of eighteen machine-gun bullets. Naturally, Escobar was the prime suspect.

By the time he met Caycedo, Jaworski said he no longer wanted a direct hand in drug trafficking. "I just made up my mind that I wasn't going to be involved with that. I was young and naive and stupid when I did it." And since pilots in the cocaine trade run the greatest risk of imprisonment, Jaworski turned Caycedo down. "I didn't want to pay the price. That's the only reason. It's not moral or ethical or any other reason. I don't think I would be able to take getting caught. For that reason, I didn't want to be involved with flying to Mexico."

Getting caught wasn't the only risk. On one trip south, Jaworski arrived at Rio Negro airport near Medellin just after a top government official had been gunned down. He had been attempting to crusade against the cartel. There were many such victims in the late 1980s as the cartel fought the Colombian state head-on. The stakes were nothing less than control of the country. Jaworski had often heard the phrase "lead or silver." It meant that drug barons would murder politicians, police officers, judges, journalists, and anyone else too honest to accept bribes or step aside. But the government official insisted on ignoring it. That was his choice, his responsibility, his problem, in cartel thinking. Caycedo was unmoved.

Jaworski never heard of Caycedo being cruel for cruelty's sake, but he was addicted to power and knew he had to keep moving forward just to stay alive. "His attitude was, 'We've been trying to reason with these people for a long time and he wouldn't listen,'" Jaworski recalled. "It was like, 'The guy got what he deserved.'"

Jaworski had no illusions that his soft-spoken boss would treat him with any more compassion if he became a problem instead of a useful ally. "Caycedo was friendly with me only because he needed me and that was it. They like to recruit American and Canadian pilots and are palsy-walsy with you. But if you get caught and thrown in jail, do you think they'd come up and foot the bill for your lawyers? You could kiss your ass good-bye. They would change their phone number and forget who you are.. You can take that to the bank."

One of Jaworski's uses was his knowledge of technical matters. His favorite reading was the "What's New" column in Popular Science, and he loved to read about new advances in science, things like alternative energy, the latest in electronics and high-tech computers. For Caycedo, such innovations translated into useful devices such as a transmitter detector the size of a pack of cigarettes that signaled the presence of police recording equipment, subtly warning its owner that undercover officers were in the area.

One evening Caycedo pulled open some maps and spread them on a metal and glass coffee table. He was in a good mood. He had a glass of Harvey's Bristol Cream, and some young women were due to arrive any moment. But something else was on his mind, and he needed Jaworski's advice. Cartel members like Caycedo constantly received visits in Medellin from people in the international drug trade, much as factories receive visits from buyers hoping to acquire products. Two Montrealers had been by in mid-1988 and had left him with a reference book listing Canadian airstrips. Caycedo pulled it out for Jaworski and pointed to a route from the mid-Atlantic and Labrador and Newfoundland. He talked about how an Israeli Astrajet might fly into Canada virtually unopposed.

"What do you think of this?" Caycedo asked, smiling.

Since an Astrajet is worth between $3 and $4 million (U.S), Jaworski's commission for arranging its sale would be between $300,000 and $400,000. Clearly, Caycedo had hooked his interest.

"When the babes finally came over, he completely ignored them," Jaworski later recalled. Instead, Caycedo seemed totally infatuated with his new eastern seaboard drug routes.

Throughout the summer of 1988, Caycedo pressured Jaworski into looking into his eastern Canadian plan. Finally, that autumn, Jaworski went to the control tower at Halifax airport, accompanied by his uncle, a former air traffic controller.

Jaworski pretended to be an innocent aircraft aficionado in a kibitzing mood. They chatted with the controllers for three hours, but within five minutes Jaworski had the information he needed. Canadian air security was lax. It would be easy to fly drug loads into the Canadian Maritimes.

"They were really nice guys," Jaworski later said of the controllers. "They didn't have a clue what I was doing."

Neither did Caycedo. This time, Jaworski was also working on a scheme of his own. The IRS hadn't been interested in cutting a deal with him back in the spring. He now needed something bigger to dangle in front of authorities.

Suddenly, the chameleon seemed to be in control.

9/ MAKING TIES

"Man, I don't know if I'm doing the right thing."

— Douglas Jaworski gets cold feet about turning informer.

THE MONDAY AFTER DOUG JAWORSKI'S VISIT, Corporal Keith Milner went to the Hamilton RCMP detachment to review Jaworski's thick file. Milner learned that Jaworski was chief officer of Florida companies with impressive names like BOHICA and AFTICA, not realizing at the time that the letters represented corporate entities like "Bend Over Here It Comes Again" and "Another Fucking Toy I Can't Afford." By the time he finished with the file, Milner was convinced Jaworski was who and what he claimed to be. "At the end of the day, it was etched into my mind that this guy was 100 percent real, no doubt about it," Milner later said.

But would Jaworski get nervous and never call back? Many potential informers backed out when it came to the crunch. Had he approached police in some other jurisdiction? Comparison shopping for the best deal was common among informers. The Drug Enforcement Administration in the United States offered informers a quarter of the value of all assets seized, but the RCMP could make no such arrangement. Could Jaworski stand being removed from criminals and the potential for huge profits? You didn't get rich working for the Mounties. Jaworski had said something about talking things over with his wife. Would she talk him out of it? Was his own family life under control?

Most informers are poor and have been charged with some crime, giving police leverage against them. They are also widely considered the bottom-feeders of the legal system, dismissed as scumbags, shit-rats, grassers, snitches, and finks, people so low they have betrayed both honest and criminal society. They run to police only at the last minute when they need help, then have the gall to act righteous and expect taxpayers' money for sending their friends to jail. And some actually expect to be treated like saviors.

But Jaworski had advantages over run-of-the-mill informers: no criminal record and no charges against him. He had no record of violence. He didn't even look capable of it. Also, he had the money to flee to another continent. With his street smarts, an obviously high IQ, and false identification, he could be living anywhere, under any name. His old standby in times of crisis or boredom was flight and it remained a strong option.

Whatever the case, Milner still had paperwork to do. There was a preliminary report to be drawn up. If ever mounted, the operation would involve a lot of people from a number of law enforcement organizations and they would need to be brought on board rapidly.

The call came December 20 — four days after they first met — when Milner was on the road. Milner's wife, Andrea, had been married to him since he graduated a decade and a half earlier from the RCMP depot in Regina. She had been through late-night calls for traffic accidents when he was a highway cop on the prairies and had endured the odd hours of his stint in the drug squad. When she could not reach her husband at the office, she alertly called Inspector Ewing to say the guy named Doug had just called.

Milner was in his squad car when the message came over the radio: "Go home as soon as possible and expect a call from your friend."

A couple of hours later, shortly after supper, Jaworski phoned again. He was extremely nervous, and his voice was unnaturally high. He said he hadn't yet explained to his wife about his involvement with the cartel.

"Man, I don't know if I'm doing the right thing," he said.

Sensing that Jaworski needed to be convinced he was making the correct move, Milner obliged. He said that when Jaworski came to the Mounties on December 16, he had taken the right path, and as long as he stayed on that road and worked with them, he was doing the right thing. But if he took off and went into hiding, he could expect a miserable life under a phony name, constantly looking over his shoulder. The alternative was to work with the RCMP, who would try to help him get his life straightened out and back under control.

Jaworski had suggested back on December 16 in his first meeting with Milner that he could help the Mounties catch key Colombians. His plan had been to set up the cartel by directing a flight into police hands. By doing this, he would rise from being simply an informer to a police operative. But he had not gone into detail.

The calls from Jaworski kept coming throughout the Christmas holidays. All had the same theme. Jaworski kept talking about his fears and doubts, and Milner kept reinforcing his decision and telling him, "You're doing the right thing. Stick with it."

The next step in setting up a sting involved a meeting with Sergeant Bob Lowe. Nicknamed the Silver Fox for his rich gray coiffure, Lowe also possessed a fox's sharp mind, which combined experience drawn from fifteen years on the drug squad with a Maritimer's no-bullshit sensibility. Tactics were Lowe's specialty, and his job on January 3, 1989, was to figure out what to make of Doug Jaworski and his wild story about life with the Medellin cartel. The site for the debriefing was a Toronto airport-strip hotel, chosen on the off chance that someone connected to the cartel might be watching Toronto Mountie headquarters at 225 Jarvis Street. It seemed paranoid, but cases and lives have been lost on smaller details.

As the meeting began, Lowe bluntly told Jaworski that he had to account for all his crimes since he left high school. If anything was left out and the Mounties later discovered it, then all deals were off. "I don't want any surprises halfway through the investigation," said Lowe.

A tape recorder was turned on so there could be no disputing what Jaworski said. No secret deals. Nothing off the record. If Jaworski was serious, he would have to get used to being monitored by strangers. It would be a controlled environment in the strictest sense of the term, and the Mounties would handle the levers.

Lowe quickly sensed that Jaworski did not like him at all, that he considered him too hard, too demanding, and too egotistical. Jaworski later said he wasn't the only person in the room skilled at getting what he wanted. "When I first met Bob Lowe, butter was melting in his mouth. He spoke of how the RCMP had had informants many, many times, and he said they received up to $500,000."

"It's difficult to do this because I feel like I'm sitting here naked," Jaworski said to the Mounties in the hotel room. Later he expanded, "It's like a card game. They want you to show your hand. But they're not offering or guaranteeing anything."

But Jaworski wasn't turning on the cartel for free. He stood to gain immunity from prosecution for crimes he admitted committing. His record might be wiped clean. He might earn a fresh, clean start and some money for his efforts. First he had to convince them that he was going to be both honest and useful. He offered the possibility of a sting, of steering the cartel into a Mountie trap. If it worked, the police could lock up key cartel figures and possibly seize money and an aircraft while gaining valuable information on how the cartel worked. If Jaworski couldn't convince the Mounties that a sting was workable, the Mounties could just record his information and say good-bye, leaving him stuck between the cartel and the IRS.

Sergeant Lowe did not recognize many of the names Jaworski mentioned, but his story had a ring of truth. The kid obviously liked to talk, something Lowe considered common to successful people, both in crime and regular business. Jaworski was clearly still nervous and did not seem to want to tell everything he knew until he got something in return, like protection, relocation, money, and a new identity. There was probably a great deal of money stashed somewhere, ready for a quick getaway and a new life. But there was no way of checking what was hidden in Panamanian or Swiss bank accounts and both sides knew it.

What exactly were Jaworski's goals? He talked about wanting to shake his problems with the Internal Revenue Service and saving his marriage. Talk of his marriage and parents seemed to trigger genuine emotions in him. He wasn't so convincing when he said he wanted to be on the right side in the fight against the illegal drug trade. The underlying reason still seemed to be that Doug Jaworski did not want to go to jail in the United States, where he was convinced the cartel had law enforcement officers on the payroll.

Sergeant Lowe began chain-smoking cigarettes when the

tape recorder was finally turned off. He was not a chatty man and smoked in silence. Jaworski was miffed. He had wanted some sort of response for his performance. It was, after all, the story of his life. "After the debriefing, Lowe just sat there and didn't say anything," Jaworski said later. "It was tough to take a tour through my background and describe my association with the cartel to people I didn't know."

Sergeant Lowe did not care whether Jaworski liked him. It was not his job to make friends, but to uphold the law. Why loosen up around a skilled manipulator? Jaworski would not have come to them if he did not need them. If he was to get a clean slate, Jaworski would have to earn it. Sergeant Lowe noted that Jaworski was curious about the hierarchy of the RCMP. In a later meeting, Lowe would notice Jaworski discreetly asking personal questions, as if trolling for information that he could later put to use to manipulate the Mounties. For that reason, Lowe decided early on that only a small group of people should have direct contact with Jaworski. But there also seemed to be a real interest on Jaworski's part in what made people do what they did, Lowe thought. To savor adventure fully, you had to understand its every nuance. "He liked to try to get into people's heads and see what made them tick," Lowe later said. "He told me a number of times that he could see both sides of things, from their perspective, from their culture."

Jaworski later said that he suspected the Mounties wanted to keep the group of handlers small so they could corner all the glory. He also explained that he wanted to understand who he was dealing with because "if somebody was going to call the shots about my life, I wanted to know who it was. They wanted to be the boss, but they didn't know what they wanted to be the boss of."

Despite his dour exterior, Sergeant Lowe found Jaworski to be a likable kid. More importantly, Lowe and others were quickly losing their skepticism about Jaworski's story. Another Mountie present, Corporal Varouj Pogharian, was fascinated by Jaworski's explanation of how small airplanes could be modified for the long nonstop flight up from Colombia to Canada. The aircraft's regular gas tanks in the wings were linked by hoses to an extra 450 gallons of fuel on board. That was more than twice as much fuel as the planes had been designed to hold, meaning they could fly at least twice as far as was normal. It was a crude and dangerous arrangement, which some pilots aggravated by smoking on board. "It's completely legitimate to say it's like a flying bomb," Jaworski later said.

That theory had been tossed about in Canadian law enforcement circles before, but no one had ever found a concrete example. Up to this point, a 50-kilo cocaine bust was considered huge by police, but small aircraft could hold more than 500 kilos. If what Jaworski was saying was true, it had enormous implications. Canada could be targeted as the next Mexico in the cartel's plans to smuggle cocaine to the American market through its neighbors.

To make the scheme work, some government, police, and court officials would have to be brought under the power of the cartel. Not all of them, just enough to keep information and drugs flowing. It seemed un-Canadian, but why not? Respect for geographic borders had never mattered to the cartel before. Why should Canada be any different from the Caribbean or South America or the southern United States? And, as the world became smaller through technology, wasn't everyone becoming neighbors?

Lowe later said, "I can remember sitting there thinking that if he was telling the truth, it would be the biggest seizure I had ever been involved in and possibly the biggest seizure this country had ever seen." Jaworski was offering the Mounties a chance to compete in the big time. First, he would give them a periscope into top levels of the cartel, to improve their knowledge. Then, he could be their torpedo, causing as much damage to the cartel's Canadian distribution system as possible. If he didn't blow up on them first....

But to make it work, Jaworski had to be able to stand up in a sting operation to draw cartel members out into the open.

Then, most importantly, he would have to play by the rules to build a solid case for Crown attorneys. If the Mounties could not gain criminal convictions, the whole exercise would be an embarrassing waste of time and money. Maybe lives too.

To gain control of the situation, the Mounties had to know who they were dealing with. Was he just a lonely, smart little kid looking for new people to play with? Was the informer role just some high-tech game of cops and robbers for him?

Was he basically a nice kid trying to right things? A boy-next-door who got in with the wrong crowd, a crowd that just happened to be the most murderous criminal group known to police? Dennis the Menace Meets Pablo Escobar?

Perhaps he was a compulsive thrill seeker, someone who would eventually get bored and complicate things just to keep them exciting.

Or maybe he was a sociopath. The term is commonly associated with cold-blooded killers, but it can apply to nonviolent deviants as well. Sociopaths are simply people without consciences. They can be bankers, journalists, police officers, actors, pilots, or drug lords. Sociopaths are impulsive, charming, pleasure-seeking, cynical, manipulative, contemptuous of authority, demanding, and ungrateful. Sociopaths put whims into action. Or they can be more normal than normal, the ultimate everyman. A true sociopath genuinely cannot understand how his or her actions hurt others. They are constant disappointments to those who get close to them and begin to expect more.

And a sociopath always lies in the end.

10/ JUMPING JACK

"Bye, bye, my darling."

— Douglas Jaworski jokingly ends telephone call
with Caycedo.

DOUG JAWORSKI WAS ON THE PHONE TO DIEGO
Caycedo, trying to calm the drug baron down. Caycedo was
anxious to put one of his boldest schemes into action. It was
January 19, 1989, and he was calling Toronto from Medellin.
Caycedo was particularly concerned about "the big piece," an
out-of-production, four-engine JetStar corporate jet. The same
kind of aircraft had been used by the villains in the James
Bond movie *Goldfinger* and now was the centerpiece of
Caycedo's "Jumping Jack Project." Cocaine would be flown
from a jungle airstrip in Colombia to a Caribbean island in an
Aero-Commander, which could handle rough jungle runways.

From there it would be loaded onto the JetStar. Its crew
would be uniformed, English-speaking, and white. Well-
dressed white passengers would also be on board, posing as
executives. Whites attracted less suspicion than native

Colombians, especially when they were carrying briefcases. Flight plans would be filed with all appropriate authorities, and the JetStar would fly directly over the United States into Pearson International Airport in Toronto. The crew and bogus executives would clear customs as the JetStar was refueled. Then they would be free to reboard and fly anywhere in Canada they wanted to deposit the 500 kilos or so of cocaine worth $250 million that was hidden deep in the jet's belly.

Possibilities without horizons would open up for Caycedo with the JetStar. It could be refueled at Goose Bay, Iceland, or Greenland, then flown over to London and the European market. Europe had yet to reach the cocaine saturation level of North America, so prices could be kept high. And Caycedo would control everything in his Jumping Jack Project, from the jungle to the capitals of Europe.

For Jaworski, there was the promise of $500,000 a flight. Originally, Caycedo had said he simply wanted Jaworski to deliver the JetStar to Colombia and teach cartel pilots how to fly it. Now, Caycedo was in a hurry. There wasn't time to teach cartel pilots.

It had cost about $80,000 for Caycedo to get the JetStar equipped with the latest in navigational equipment. Now he wanted to be paid back for his investment in a big way. Caycedo had others to answer to and Jaworski was holding things up. Caycedo's job was like that of a broker. Once he had an operational plan, a half dozen suppliers might agree to use his operations, much like investors throwing their money into a mutual fund. This way, nobody would be totally compromised in the event of a disaster, while everyone could share in success. This arrangement also meant that many top Colombians besides Caycedo were extremely anxious for Jaworski to get things moving in Canada. Because of its European element, the scheme would have to involve contact with traditional Italian Mafia elements overseas. The Mafia had easy access to heroin from the Golden Triangle of Southeast Asia, and trades of their heroin for Colombian cocaine were already under way.

On the phone, Caycedo was clearly impatient, and for good reason. The Canadian had a mind of his own and insisted on doing things at his own pace, if he did them at all. Jaworski explained in English that he was trying to buy property, set up a hangar, pay necessary taxes, and get his phone set up.

Caycedo: Listen, let's get to work. You're wasting too much time.

Jaworski: Yeah, I know. I've had problems. You know that.

Caycedo: Yeah, but this is a new year and you got to look in another way.

Jaworski: Well, that's why I'm here now and I'm calling you, and I'm here now for good....

Unknown to Caycedo, the Mounties were taping the call. For the first time, they could hear the voice of their quarry. It was heavily accented, friendly, and yet guarded. Caycedo communicated in clipped sentences, not because he could not think or speak fluently, but because he was constantly aware of wiretaps and potential treachery. He owned a complex descrambler system that played havoc with police microphones, but this time it wasn't turned on. He was either arrogant, careless, or too trusting of his friend Jaworski.

The Mounties knew even before they heard the voice that it would be virtually impossible to extradite from Colombia someone at Caycedo's level. When Colombian officials had pushed for extraditions in 1986, cartel leaders had responded with a wave of assassinations and bombings that had terrified Colombia's Supreme Court and nullified the extradition treaty.

Extradition was an admission that Colombia's jails and judicial system could not handle the drug barons. It was also the ultimate insult to drug lords, many of whom aspired to barge their way into their country's oligarchy, following the path of the ruthless coffee barons who had built fortunes while operating out of Medellin a century before. The Mounties knew there were limits to what Canadian police could expect. They would have to content themselves with identifying and targeting people in Canada who were importing cocaine at the 100- to 500-kilo level.

As he chatted with Caycedo, Jaworski suddenly realized he was playing the role of police agent. The sensation surprised him. "It was like I threw a switch. I remember feeling completely oblivious to everything that was going on around me. I was completely focused on what I was trying to accomplish. As soon as I hung up, it switched again. I just had to kind of develop [the skill] as I went along. There was no way to practice."

The Mounties could see the kid was clearly a good liar. He stalled Caycedo, saying he needed to find technically competent help and that the JetStar was being held up because of maintenance problems. In reality, the Mounties were not yet ready to go ahead and put their trust in Jaworski. Also they wanted arrests in Canada, and chasing the JetStar could divert them to Europe. It would be tough enough to keep things under control in Canada. "There were a lot of manipulations going on everywhere," Jaworski later said. "He was trying to manipulate me and I was trying to manipulate him. That was going to be constant and ongoing. Then you get the Mounties in there. Then you get my wife in there. Everybody was manipulating everybody."

Jaworski took some of the edge off Caycedo's mood by asking his boss to eat some food from Medellin's posh Monserrat Restaurant for him. Caycedo frequently ordered out from Monserrat, finding the security details of dining at a restaurant in person too much of a bother.

"All right, every time I do, I remember you." Caycedo laughed. "Okay, take care."

"Bye, bye, my darling," Jaworski replied gently. He knew pretending they were gay lovers was guaranteed a laugh every time in the macho world of the cartel. It was so outlandish, so ridiculous, so contrary to their images, that no other response was possible. It was also simultaneously affectionate and a statement that he was not of their world, but just a perceptive, tough-to-handle visitor.

A few days later, Jaworski was at Pearson International Airport in Toronto working on the JetStar executive jet he had just tricked Caycedo into delivering north. Jaworski was concentrating on getting the JetStar's fourth engine working, when a stranger approached with Corporal Keith Milner. Jaworski already had a favorable impression of Milner, nicknaming him "Maple Syrup and Ice Cream," for his clean-cut, all-Canadian good looks and jockish demeanor. Milner would be a good person to troll bars looking for girls with, were they both single and fancy-free, Jaworski thought.

Jaworski didn't pay them much attention when they climbed into the back of the plane, apparently waiting for him to come back and talk. About fifteen minutes later, the engine was idling and it was too loud in the cockpit to think. Jaworski got up from the pilot's seat and shut the outside door.

The stairs to the tarmac automatically retracted.

When Jaworski glanced back into the aircraft, he saw terror in the eyes of the stranger and Milner.

"You're not taking this thing up?" one of them asked.

Had Jaworski snapped? Was this a sick joke? The police had been wary about Jaworski figuratively taking them for a ride. Was he now about to literally do just that? Where to? Colombia? What for? Murder? Ransom? Torture?

"No, no, I'm testing the engines," Jaworski replied.

Realizing he had been rude to ignore his visitors, Jaworski walked back to meet Milner and the stranger, whom Milner introduced as Sergeant Wayne Umansky. An undercover ace for the Mounties, Umansky was a star in a style of acting that allowed for no second takes or editing. Death, not negative reviews, was the result of a bad performance on Umansky's stage.

Umansky was a large, powerful man with a presence that somehow made him seem bigger still. But strangely, when he wanted to, he could blend into a situation so completely that experienced surveillance teams might lose him on a city street. Umansky certainly did not look like a cop, let alone one with a reputation for being meticulous with paperwork. He also had a tough appearance that was totally absent in Jaworski. "He looked like a guy who'd skin you alive if you crossed him," Jaworski thought.

They chatted briefly, then Jaworski asked if they were in the mood for a spin around Ontario.

"No, no, no, it's okay," the Mounties said.

Umansky let loose with a deep laugh that seemed to start at the soles of his feet and build up in force as it rumbled toward his mouth. Jaworski liked people who laughed a lot and Umansky seemed to enjoy his black humor.

Maybe that was something for both the Mounties and Jaworski to build upon. The Mounties had not yet made any commitment to take part in the sting. But if they did, Umansky would be part of it and he and Jaworski would have to be able to feed off each other intuitively while meeting the enemy face to face.

11/ THE UNKNOWN

"You know we don't like to depend on anybody, right?"

— Diego Caycedo on his business.

AS JAWORSKI AND THE MOUNTIES SLEPT, SIRENS wailed at 3:45 in the morning on January 24, 1989, at a United States Air Force base in Loring, Maine. What the American air force labeled an "unknown" had penetrated American air space and crews scrambled to battle stations.

Within minutes, two fully armed F-15 fighter planes were heading faster than the speed of sound on a course that would put them online with the intruder in just a few minutes. Whatever the unknown was, it had not punched in a computer code to identify itself to a transponder on the ground that monitored aircraft. The unknown had filed no flight plan and ignored all attempts to establish radio contact. It might be a plane in distress or a missile or a Soviet fighter plane heading toward the Canadian border or a plane full of $250 million of cocaine.

The single-seat F-15s flew single file up to 37,000 feet and locked their radar onto the unknown, a faint blip some fifty or sixty miles away. They shot past the unknown at 950 to 1,000 miles an hour, then circled back to just twelve miles behind the pilot. Flying an F-15 was like sitting on a rocket, trying to harness raw power, and the fighter pilots found themselves frustrated by the unknown's slow speed. The pilots had to veer off to the right and circle back to keep from crashing over the back of whatever it was ahead of them, now heading north at 250 miles an hour into the dark. It was too cloudy to get a look, but whatever it was had no lights and gave off no radio messages.

The fighter planes circled back again, then came within five miles of it. Normally, the F-15s' high-intensity lighting gave a full fifteen miles of visibility at night, but it was cloudy and the unlighted unknown remained a mystery. The trailing F-15 hung back, ready to pounce if someone inside opened fire.

The three aircraft were leaving American air space, and the fighter pilots switched radio frequencies to make contact with Canadian air traffic controllers. The F-15s spun back for a third time, then the lead plane pulled up low at 1,500 feet to the right of the unknown. Still the fighter pilot could see nothing.

The lead F-15 slid back, then approached high and to the left. Still nothing. Then it dropped low and to the left. Stars above it were blacked out. The radar was right. Something was flying up there. The lead F-15 dropped low and to the right for a better look and flashed its brilliant red beacons at what appeared to be an aircraft fuselage above it.

No response. As the F-15 continued to flash its beacons, the unknown seemed to fly progressively slower. The lead F-15 pulled up to between just 50 and 100 feet of the unknown's wing tip, and a scant 20 feet below it. It would have been extremely dangerous for cars to tailgate this closely on the freeway. In the pitch black, moving at 250 miles an hour, the risk was far greater.

Now they were formation flying and still strangers. The F-15 edged to within ten feet of its flying prey, then switched on its white, green, and red lights, so that it now resembled a high-speed Christmas tree. The lights could usually be seen from fifteen miles. Finally, the F-15 pilot got a clean look at the unknown. What he saw was a tan or off-white twin-engine turboprop aircraft with the letters C GJNH on its side. The "C" would represent the initial of the country of registration for the aircraft, presumably Canada. Under the lights, he could now see that the "C" was a little smaller and more blockish than the other letters, as if it had somehow been doctored. Near the letters was a tiny maple leaf.

The turboprop seemed big enough to seat a dozen people, or to carry 500 kilos of cocaine and enough extra fuel to power it from Colombia. Air traffic controllers told the F-15 pilot to give hand signals to the turboprop, to see if it was in trouble. Still there was no response. The maneuvers would have been dangerous if they knew each other. But they were strangers. From the attitude of the pilot of the unknown, they were probably enemies too. The F-15 pilot, an eighteen-year air force veteran, later said he had never come up against a pilot as brash and arrogant as whoever was at the unknown's controls.

An F-15 can fly 2.5 times the speed of sound, but it also burns fuel rapidly. The lead pilot called down to see if a military 707 tanker could be dispatched to transfer fuel to it midair. Instead, the fighter planes were instructed to head back to Loring. The lead F-15 did a quick climb, then flipped upside down, so its pilot could glimpse the turboprop trail away in the direction of Trois-Rivières, Quebec, disappearing into the dark.

The military pilots chasing the plane had done well but

they couldn't know what it all meant: Diego Caycedo had already started flying cocaine into Canada. The Mounties had to catch up or be left behind.

Caycedo said nothing about the F-15 drama when, on January 27, he again prodded Jaworski to hurry up. A thirteen-hour flight to Canada meant hundreds of millions of dollars and Caycedo wanted to get things going. They spoke on the phone in an easily deciphered code: Toronto was Thomas, Montreal was Mom, 500,000 dollars was 500, planes were pieces or cars, and pilots were drivers. Caycedo often concocted the codes as he went along, speaking in clipped, cautious semi-sentences.

Caycedo wanted details of what hangars and facilities Jaworski planned to buy in the Maritimes. The Colombian kept pushing Jaworski to double- and triple-check his work, causing at least one Mountie to wonder if Jaworski was as close to the drug lord as he had claimed.

Caycedo: Can you get a fax over there and organize yourself for a change?

Jaworski: That's what I'm working on, pal.

Caycedo: Yeah, but you're taking too long.

Jaworski: You always say that, but I'm by myself. I don't have fifty guys that can go and get me sandwiches and do things for me.

Jaworski's remark loosened up Caycedo, who, of course, did have fifty men to get him sandwiches and do his bidding. Caycedo laughed, "I can send you a few if you want." Any helpers sent north should come equipped "with big tits," Jaworski joked. He could not explain that he felt he was being slowed down by cash-strapped Mounties, who could not yet get clearance to rent a fax machine.. As the conversation wound down, Caycedo took a break from business and they talked about women. Caycedo did not just like the company of women, he also greatly enjoyed bragging about them.

Caycedo: I got something for you here.. You wouldn't believe it when you come back. I mean, really gorgeous.

Jaworski: You're not going to fall in love again, are you?

Caycedo: No, no. I never do. (Laughs)

Jaworski: You did so. You were moping around for three weeks the last time.

Caycedo: (Laughs) Yeah, which one was that?

Jaworski: Oh, I don't remember the names.

Caycedo: You know something? Uh, remember the one with the beautiful hair?

Jaworski: Yeah.

Caycedo: Keeps calling all the time. I just don't answer any more. (Laughs)

Caycedo kept pushing while Jaworski continued to make excuses, saying that things were complicated, that he had to arrange to get a copilot to fly the JetStar, that he did not have enough help, and that his shaky marriage needed time to mend.

Caycedo made it clear that none other than Pablo Escobar — referred to by one of his nicknames of Peter — was impatient too. When Escobar got edgy and impatient, the mood was infectious, even fatal.

"Do me a favor," Caycedo asked. "Fax me enough information about it because Peter keeps asking me about the big piece [JetStar]. We're losing money."

As the conversation wound down, Caycedo said he would like Jaworski to go down to Colombia for a visit and to update Caycedo on his Canadian operations. They talked of mixing business with hunting at the new jungle home Caycedo was having built.

But on February 2, Caycedo still didn't have the papers he

wanted and was still clearly impatient. He let Jaworski know that a competitor was setting up a rival base. And he told Jaworski that he could make lots of money if he hurried, saying, "I'm gonna have so much work for you, you wouldn't believe it."

What Caycedo did not spell out was exactly why he needed new airstrips when he was already landing planes in Sorel, near Montreal. Sorel had been phase one of the operation, an experiment to see if flights into eastern Canada were viable. For the Sorel test runs, Caycedo had used Hell's Angels and members of Montreal's West End Gang of Anglo thugs to set up an airstrip and unload planes. The operation had been a success.

But in order to make real money, Caycedo knew he had to cut out such middlemen and control the operation from start to finish. He did not want another Mexico situation, where he was forced to rely upon corrupt intermediaries who were not firmly under his power.

Caycedo liked frequent telephone calls from his workers, so that he could move them about like chess pieces. When someone did not call back regularly or move quickly enough, Caycedo simply worked around them. He did not have to threaten people. Ignoring them and cutting them out of huge potential profits was punishment enough.

Caycedo: You know we don't like to depend on anybody, right?

Jaworski: Yeah, not even me. (Laughs)

Caycedo: We can't afford to.

Jaworski: I understand.

Caycedo: You see, it's like having an industry and you're depending on a few guys and the industry stops because the guys are not around. We just cannot let it happen. It happen to us too many times.

For the Mounties, it was an education. Their quarry was clearly smart, adaptable, rich, and already flooding Canada with huge amounts of cocaine. And this was only the starting point for Caycedo. Whether the Mounties could even put a small dent in his plans remained to be seen. When one member of the Mountie team placed a $5 bet on whether the operation would succeed, he was given fifty-fifty odds.

12/ TROUBLE AT HOME

"I loved her more than anything in the world."

— Douglas Jaworski struggles to save his marriage while
duping the cartel.

SOMETHING HAD TO BE DONE TO GET
Jaworski's private life under control. First, he called his parents,
who still lived in the British Virgin Islands. "They had to be
informed, in case anything happened," Jaworski recalled. "Also,
I needed their support."

The story his parents heard on the telephone cast Jaworski
in the light of a crime-buster. His father would later recall
that Doug was very emotional, saying, "Dad, they're going to
take this stuff into my country. And they're not going to do
it. I'm going to stop them."

"I'll support you 100 percent," Reg Jaworski replied, with
no idea how that one sentence would forever change his life
and the lives of the rest of his family. Doug Jaworski had lived
on his own since he was eighteen. Now he would be coming
back into their lives in a very big — and horrifying — way.

Jaworski said that his parents knew that his clients included the cartel, but then stayed out of his business. "My dad has always said, 'I have never gotten involved with your business.' That means that he never asked me about it. He listened when I talked but that was it. And it was very seldom that I talked."

Explaining things to Susan would be far tougher. They had already had serious disputes over money, and Jaworski refused to merge bank accounts with her even after marriage. During one trip to Switzerland, he made her wait outside while he handled his finances at a bank. "Susan was funny about money," Jaworski later said. "Maybe I was too."

Despite their problems, Jaworski still loved her and respected her intelligence. But she liked order, while Jaworski thrived on life at the edge. In more ways than one, they lived in different worlds; Jaworski said, "When I'd fly to South America, I'd be surrounded by people who were basically indigent — very poor — and then I'd come home the same day, exhausted, and Susan would be absolutely pissed that I forgot to bring a gallon of milk home. I'd see people who were basically starving and the corruption of Colombia itself — no matter what you want to do, you have to make little bribe payments to everybody. Then I'd come home and there was no way to explain what I'd seen and done that day. What did I do? I just got in the car and got the milk."

Susan flew north to Canada for the lunch. She met Corporal Keith Milner at the waterside Pat and Mario's in Burlington near Toronto. It was Milner's job to tell her what Jaworski's cooperation with police would mean to her life. She could expect to lose her job, name, and other normal trappings of life. Her history would be altered and she would have to move out of familiar surroundings. Visits with old friends and loved ones would have to be carefully managed. In a sense, she would have to die, then be reborn somewhere else.

Unless, of course, the cartel caught hold of the news. Everyone who read the Miami *Herald* knew about what happened to informers, knew about Colombian neckties.

A half dozen times, Susan left their table in tears. Each time she returned from the washroom, she fought to keep her composure and failed again.

During one of her absences, Jaworski turned to Milner and said, "This is going to be a tough nut to crack."

Jaworski felt he could switch his undercover act on and off like a light switch. Susan had an equally strong personality, but could not regulate her emotions so easily. As Jaworski said, "She could turn it on and off, but not at will. I didn't see it as a complete black hole of badness. I saw opportunities here. I mean, enough money to live off the interest and not have to work. To be able to start a family and be together and not have to worry about a lot of things that a lot of people have to worry about otherwise. She didn't want to hear about that. She just wanted to hear about how bad it was and how terrible it was going to be. And I was sad about that. I couldn't understand why it was having such a bad effect on her."

Milner later recalled, "It's not a pleasant future. You're sitting there and you're very proud of your family name and you realize that you're going to lose your name. You're going to lose your employment. You have to move to another locale. You have to accept that to visit your parents, or trusted friends, you have to meet at a third-party location."

The meeting lasted about two hours. As they left the restaurant, Susan looked at Milner and said meekly, "Take care of him."

"We will," Milner replied.

Jaworski rolled his eyes and thought to himself, "She was playing it to the hilt, just like I knew she would. Old Sympathy Susan."

When it was over, Jaworski drove her back to the airport

to fly back to Florida. "The ride to the airport was just brutal," Jaworski said.

"Why didn't you tell me this stuff before we got married?" she asked.

"You knew," Jaworski told her.

With that, Susan flew to her empty home, even more worried than she had been when she arrived in Toronto earlier in the day.

But she still had an emotional hold over Jaworski. Maybe it wasn't too late to talk him out of the sting.

13/ FALL FROM FAVOR

"You know, people tell me things."

— Diego Caycedo lets Doug Jaworski know he is
being watched.

DIEGO CAYCEDO COULDN'T HAVE BEEN HAPPIER.

"We hit it three times in a row and it went beautiful," he
said on the long-distance telephone line between Medellin
and Toronto on February 3.

Three flights into Canada within the past two weeks had
arrived safely. That meant Caycedo had imported some $750
million of cocaine right under the noses of Jaworski and the
police.

And things were just getting started.

Jaworski and the Mounties had known about only one of
the three flights, the one the U.S. Air Force had followed.

Jaworski was stunned. Later, he described his thoughts:
"Three times! Three times! They had only been intercepted
once."

Someone in the intelligence section of Ottawa headquarters noticed, in the daily tide of paperwork, a report filed by the American F-15 pilot about the January 24 air chase. It read a lot like the scenario that informer Doug Jaworski had outlined and the report was forwarded to Toronto. Suddenly, Jaworski's credibility shot up with the force... just as Caycedo stopped needing him so badly.

After the February 3 call, events started to come into focus for Jaworski and the Mounties.

Caycedo had been pushing Jaworski to set up an airstrip, using the sale of airplanes as bait. There was a potential $1 million (U.S.) in sales commissions altogether. Caycedo sought a half dozen King-Air 200s, the same aircraft that would have made the Quebec flights, and also little Cessna 206s, the "Bolivian Specials" that were so useful for short hauls. The King-Airs would let Caycedo crank up flights, now that the route Jaworski had helped design was a proven winner. He planned to have one fly to Canada, refuel, return to Colombia, then switch pilots, add more fuel and cocaine, and repeat the process immediately. When this King-Air returned, another would do the same thing while the first plane was serviced. That way Caycedo could get maximum use out of his ground crews, aircraft, and fronts of good weather. The Cessnas would move cocaine from warehouses to buyers across Canada and the United States.

The intercepted flight to Sorel had just been an experiment for Caycedo as he tested the radar on the Atlantic corridor. The Sorel runway was already controlled by the mysterious Raoul of the cartel and it was expensive for Caycedo to use it. Now, Caycedo wanted his own airstrip. It was time to make really big money.

But he wasn't about to depend on Jaworski to provide it for him.

There was always someone like Sonny, a cartel worker who continually wore a smile that said, "Damn, today's the day I make my fortune."

Now pushing sixty, Sonny might have finally been right. That bonanza might be realized at a tiny, dirt airstrip about twenty miles outside Albany, New York. A plane could get there following the same Atlantic route as would be used for the Maritimes or Quebec, with a sharp left just before they got into Canada.

Sonny had a little band of white-trash law breakers who all looked as if they just fell off the back of a pickup truck in the hills of Georgia. "You could tell by the dirt on their clothes that they hadn't seen a washing machine for quite a while," Jaworski said. "When they walked around, it was like they were sneaking around."

Caycedo had used Sonny and his men in the past when he wanted a fresh stock of compact Uzi assault rifles. He had pressured Jaworski for some too, saying they would come in handy for fighting leftist guerrillas some day. But Jaworski said he declined, instead flying down a gift of a $200 shotgun, which Jaworski promptly borrowed for duck hunting at Caycedo's ranch. If you were caught with an Uzi in Colombia, it was far worse than a cocaine conviction. Even Pablo Escobar might be in trouble for that, which explained why Caycedo and the bodyguard generally wore only .38 revolvers. But Sonny and his crew jumped at the chance to make $150 or so per Uzi from Caycedo. They ordered a couple of dozen from a gun shop in Pompano Beach, Florida. Stupidly, they lied on the registration forms, saying they didn't have criminal records.

Naturally, they were arrested. This had given Caycedo headaches, but Sonny was still useful to have around. Especially now, when the Atlantic route looked viable and Jaworski appeared unmanageable. Instead Jaworski was dispatched by Caycedo to critique Sonny's latest handiwork, the airstrip near Albany.

What he saw made Jaworski panic. Sonny had apparently spent $15,000 (U.S.) setting it up. The runway was long and well packed, and gas supplies were on hand. Sonny was prepared to receive drugs now.

Jaworski still hadn't even found an airstrip. If Caycedo started using the Albany airstrip, he would no longer need Jaworski. That meant the American Drug Enforcement Administration might get to make the bust, not the Mounties. And Jaworski's plan to use Canadian police to solve his IRS problem would be dead, since he had yet to sign a deal with them. Word might leak out that he had spoken to police. Suddenly he could tumble from being an undercover agent to being a two-time loser, tossed out on his own to sort out his own problems.

"Sonny was ready to go," Jaworski later said. "Everything was set up and ready to go. All of a sudden, the whole deal with Canada would go down the toilet. I hadn't spent a month and a half with the Mounties up in Canada to have it handed to the DEA in one day. I had no idea that Sonny was even close to doing anything like this."

It is standard for the cartel to use rivals to critique each other's work. That way they are guaranteed a tough assessment that overlooks no flaws. To balance things, Caycedo also dispatched his brother Fausto from Miami; senior cartel pilot Jose Ali Galindo-Escobar of Colombia, better known as Jay; and Juan, a DC-3 owner from Colombia who flew chemicals and coca paste. Now Juan wanted to move up to the big leagues and big money — and "become an international man," the dream of every cartel pilot. They surveyed Sonny's airstrip for the length and firmness of the runway and availability of fuel.

It passed on all counts. Sonny had done his work well. Perhaps he would finally make his fortune.

Jaworski drifted into a conversation with Jay, the pilot. The Colombian had a reputation for doing yeoman service flying cocaine into Mexico and must have made millions of dollars from the cartel by the time he was in his late thirties. Jay had invested in a fertilizer company. He should have been able to support himself comfortably in a legitimate way.

"Why don't you quit?" Jaworski asked.

"No money," the pilot replied.

As they surveyed Sonny's work, Jaworski became increasingly depressed. He grumbled that Caycedo owed him money, then he walked away from the rest of the pilots. And when they organized an aerial inspection with the other pilots — as Caycedo had requested — Jaworski simply packed up and left for Canada.

Plans for a Canadian sting seemed over before it even began.

Diego Caycedo was furious. "You complain a lot!" he shouted into the phone. Caycedo constantly checked up on his workers and did not like what he had heard about Jaworski's moodiness in Albany. Caycedo expected the people he was making rich to show some semblance of loyalty.

"People tell me things, you know," Caycedo continued. It was February 7, and he was calling long distance between Medellin and Fredericton. "I mean, they hear them, they gotta tell me things... and that's pretty bad, that you sound so unhappy every time you talk to my people. I think you ought to have a good conversation with me and tell me whatever you must tell me, don't you think?"

This time, there was no opportunity for Jaworski to be glib and laugh it off.

"You don't know how much I despise to have my workers saying that somebody else is complaining about money, complaining about work, complaining about not getting what he must get," Caycedo lectured. "I mean, that's pretty bad for me, you know. It makes me sound like shit."

That day, Jaworski and the Mounties went all out, trying to set up an airstrip for the sting. They surveyed nine airstrips by helicopter. Jaworski's instructions from Caycedo had been to find an airstrip east of Montreal. New Brunswick offered a number of small runways that had been used for budworm spraying. The best facility for Caycedo's purposes was in the northern wilderness at tiny Troutbrook. Second was Wayman Field near Fredericton. Troutbrook offered an easy-to-navigate 5,000-foot runway, compared to just 2,700 feet for Wayman. But Troutbrook presented logistical problems for the Mounties. Where would all the undercover officers necessary for a sting operation stay? How would they be fed? There was an RCMP helicopter in Fredericton, just a short flight from Wayman. Troutbrook was in the middle of nowhere.

Caycedo had to be sold on Wayman, if he was still interested at all. Jaworski decided to play on Caycedo's cheapness. Back when Jaworski was selling airplanes and parts to the multimillionaire, he always padded any bill over $50,000 by $2,000. That way, Caycedo always got the satisfaction of haggling it down $2,000 while Jaworski received his desired selling price. Now, Jaworski planned to tell Caycedo the asking price for Troutbrook was $400,000, and that it could probably be bought for $350,000. Jaworski set Wayman's asking price at $250,000 and probable selling price at $200,000. "I knew he'd go for the cheap one," Jaworski reasoned.

But Sonny's work near Albany meant it might be too late for Jaworski's tricks.

Later that night, it was Susan's turn to yell at Jaworski. A Mountie down the hallway in Jaworski's Fredericton hotel could hear him shouting into the telephone receiver during his nightly call to Florida. The Mountie wasn't surprised; by now long-distance screaming was the norm, not the exception.

Even Jaworski was unhappy with himself. "My new attempt at being an undercover operator was a dismal failure in the eyes of everybody, including myself. If I was going to continue with this project, I would have to get a helluva lot better at being undercover and I'd have to do it fast."

Jaworski fantasized every day about fleeing everything and flying off to Europe. "It was coming closer and closer to reality. I was very capable of getting on an airplane in five minutes. I had it all organized. I organized it before I ever got involved in this. But the marriage was not gone. I promised myself that I would give it my best shot, and giving it my best shot did not mean quitting after the first strikeout."

The next time Caycedo and Jaworski talked, Caycedo picked up his long-distance lecture where he had left off. "I just can't take complaints, you know. I don't like them." Then he turned sarcastic, saying, "You never made a penny with me. I don't know how you survive." After a long pause, Caycedo gathered himself and continued, "When you get to the point where I am now, that you have your own cars [planes] and that you have your own merchandise [cocaine] and you have your own drivers [pilots] and that you risk, everything, yourself, you will find out that the rest of people when they do something for you, they make some money for it, but they don't make all the money that you make, because you are the one who's risking everything that there is to be able to get the operation successful."

By February 10, Caycedo seemed to have cooled down. He urged Jaworski to fly down to Medellin to talk things out and update him on New Brunswick. Caycedo noted that the Canadian operation was of keen interest at the top level of the cartel, referring to Pablo Escobar by his nickname Peter and saying, "Make sure you bring me papers and things so I read and see what it is about. Because you know, I gotta show my partner Peter also about those things and let him know, you know, what's happening."

Caycedo's final request was rich in irony. He had tons of

extremely expensive and illegal drugs in his home country, but yearned for a few bottles of Harvey's Bristol Cream, a sherry easily available to anyone of legal drinking age in North America.

"Nobody has brought any to me in four months or six months," he said.

14/ ONE DEGREE HOTTER

"I knew the end was near."

— Douglas Jaworski returns to Colombia.

SOME THINGS NEVER SEEMED TO CHANGE IN Medellin, like the petroleum stink that hung in the air. Medellin was boxed in on all sides by the Andes mountains. Cars and trucks had to strain to make it out, leaving their fumes trapped at the base of the mountains by a lack of wind. The problem was made worse by the high-octane fumes spewed out from each vehicle, in a land where anti-pollution filters were all but unknown. That stink had always bothered Jaworski, who was disgusted even by a whiff of cigarette smoke. The weather was always the same too — just a little chilly — a combination of its mountain location and proximity to the equator. Yet another constant was the all-pervasive feeling of cartel corruption. Jaworski had never liked coming into Medellin even when he was Caycedo's friend. White North Americans were always suspected of being agents from the Drug Enforcement Administration and, as such, were prime candidates for murder.

The Colombian trip posed a dilemma for the Mounties. Without it, the operation would be dead. But carrying on could kill Jaworski. However, Jaworski had still not officially signed any agreement with the RCMP. Like anyone else, he was free to go to Colombia if he wished.

The Mounties knew they could not tell anyone in Colombia that Jaworski was coming. Any small leak in security would kill him. All information had to be tightly controlled.

"He had an awful lot of balls to go down there," said Staff Sergeant Allan MacDonald. "We knew he was taking an awful risk."

Jaworski was oddly fascinated by the situation, later describing his actions almost as if he were viewing another person. "I was right at the point where I had absolutely nothing left to give. I was stressed out to the maximum. I just felt that emotionally I wasn't going to be able to make it any farther. But every time I felt that way, the temperature got one degree hotter. It was amazing. Absolutely amazing....

"I knew the end was near. So I wanted to clean up my accounts with him. He owed me and I went down there with the idea that I was going to beg, buy, borrow, and steal as much as I can from this sonofabitch, because when the end finally comes, he's going to try to kill me, so I might as well take what I can get."

The standard $400 (U.S.) slipped to an airport official allowed Jaworski to pass through immigration without having his passport stamped. Too many Colombian stamps on a passport looked suspicious, and an airport worker had gone through this ritual with Jaworski numerous times in the past. One of

Diego Caycedo's bodyguards was waiting outside, and he took Jaworski on the one-hour, fifteen-minute drive to Caycedo's best safehouse on a hill looking down on the city.

They passed through the black wrought-iron fence that surrounded the luxury condominium complex. It had always seemed odd that an old security guard with a long-nosed .38 stood watch there, supposedly protecting some of the most dangerous criminals in the world. He was useful, though. When cartel members worried their phones might be bugged, they slipped down to the guardhouse to conduct business on his phone. The guard's pants were a couple of sizes too big, his hat was dirty, and he invariably wore a sweater to shield him against Medellin's chill. In Medellin, a full set of teeth was a luxury reserved for only the rich and the young, and the guard was neither.

Another bodyguard received Jaworski at the front door and pointed him upstairs, where Caycedo was seated on a black leather couch, ready to do business. Caycedo seemed happy to see him, but Jaworski could not shake the feeling that he was being set up. Caycedo always knew more than he said. He had to. His survival depended on knowledge. Even now, Jaworski did not dislike Caycedo, despite the tongue-lashing on the phone and the plotting with the police. In an odd way, Jaworski could not help feeling somewhat pleased that his old buddy was happy.

"This was the best thing that had ever happened for him. They were going to make more out of this. They were already spending it. I was convinced that they knew I was working for the feds. I was convinced, even though they didn't.

"I was paranoid through the trip but somehow I made it and I actually had fun while I was down there. It was nice to see him and talk to him and know how sneaky I was being. And Diego's such a nice guy and he was in such a good mood. It was like, anything you wanted, you could get....

"I didn't think that they knew [about the sting], but in another part of me, I was just scared shitless that — if they ever found out — I'd never get out alive. That would just be it. It would just be like a ginsu knife that would slice and dice in a million different ways — worm food."

Caycedo phoned Jay, his friend and senior pilot, and told him to come over immediately. Then he pulled out his maps, too excited to wait for Jay's arrival. Jaworski's role was to act as a salesman, telling Caycedo that New Brunswick's airports were closer to Colombia than anywhere else in Canada. For Caycedo, that meant less fuel and room for 600 instead of 500 kilos of cocaine. Since pilots were paid by the flight and not cargo size, this was a valuable cost-saver.

Jay arrived shortly, and Jaworski backtracked to explain the plan to him. He seemed impressed also. Then Jaworski took out a phony land sales advertisement for Wayman Field and glossy overhead pictures of the tiny airstrip, taken from the RCMP helicopter.

Caycedo's face tightened. Something was wrong.

"They're the same," he said, gesturing to the picture in the advertisement and the photo from the helicopter.

He was right. The bogus ad and the photos were the work of Jaworski and the Mounties. It was a small error but a potentially fatal one. Less than an hour into the deception and already Caycedo had caught him in a lie.

Jaworski tried to shrug it off, saying that his team hired the same company to take the aerial shots as the advertiser had. Caycedo seemed to believe it. If not, then Jaworski wasn't the only good actor in the room.

Jay also didn't look upset. One successful flight into Wayman Field would net him $500,000 (U.S.) and another $150,000 for his copilot. It was easy to think about the money and forget the dangers. Especially when you felt you needed the money.

Caycedo called Pablo Escobar and set up a meeting for the next day, knowing that Jaworski was always uneasy in Colombia and did not want to stay any longer than was absolutely necessary.

Alex signaled the end of the regular business day by escorting in three disturbingly gorgeous women. But Caycedo still wanted to talk business. Jaworski said he could get the Wayman Field operation working in two weeks. Caycedo countered sarcastically that this probably meant two to three months. "I knew at that point that, come hell or high water, I would be ready in two weeks," Jaworski later said. "The RCMP seemed to be on my side now. Diego was preoccupied with the Albany airstrip, but for that flight, they would have to stop in St. Kitts. They had trouble with that before because the air traffic controllers and fuel people were inherently unreliable. Fuel availability was sporadic and they hadn't commandeered the air traffic control system of St. Kitts — just a couple of individuals. The right guys had to be working."

Caycedo said he could probably get Jaworski some Canadian cash or traveler's cheques, if that would speed things up. The money could be withdrawn in Panama on his way back to Canada. Jaworski said he could pick it up in Montreal instead, since the cartel was having troubles moving drug profits out of Quebec. Ironically, it was often easier to get the dope into a country than the money out. Jaworski tried to be accommodating, realizing that by picking up the cash he would help flush out some of the cartel's Montreal organization. Before police could attack it, they had to find it. Caycedo took the bait and threw in an extra $100,000 to see if Jaworski could help laundering it.

Jaworski kept trying to push Caycedo away from the Albany project. The best they could hope for there was a 65 percent chance of success, he said, compared to 95 percent for New Brunswick. Jay said he didn't like the risks of the American route either. Then business talk ceased for the night. It was time for Alex's girls.

The maid had just finished serving breakfast the next morning when Caycedo started talking business again. He needed everything clear in his head before the noon meeting with Pablo Escobar. There seemed to be no way flights into New Brunswick would be caught. Caycedo also had thought of a way to sneak planes from New Brunswick across the American border into upper New York State. Cocaine-laden planes would suddenly drop low from 25,000 feet over Yarmouth, Nova Scotia, and keep flying north. At Princeton, Maine, the crew would radio a cartel plane on the ground that had already filed a flight plan to Albany. The two planes would piggyback a short distance before the second plane landed and the cocaine-filled plane continued on its flight plan. Jaworski was impressed with the scheme to beat radar coverage, but argued it had no better than a 75 percent chance of success. Odds for success at Albany were 92 percent, compared to 98 or 99 percent for New Brunswick, in Caycedo's opinion.

The pilots and Caycedo left to meet with Escobar, and suddenly Jaworski was alone.

The only time Jaworski left the condominium during his three-day visit was when he went out that afternoon to see his old friend, Pinguino. His real name was Fernando Augusto Mendoza-Jaramillo, but everyone in the cartel who knew him called him Pinguino because he rocked side to side when he walked, like a penguin. Pinguino didn't seem to mind the nickname. He was just happy to be part of the club.

Pinguino had come a long way since he and Jaworski first met a year before, when Jaworski was delivering his first plane to Caycedo and Pinguino lacked the confidence to land it by himself. Back then — just a year earlier — Pinguino's forte was flying in smuggled goods such as stereos and televisions from Panama and bypassing customs duties. Since then,

Pinguino had made $450,000 (U.S.) as the copilot on the three flights into Sorel.

Pinguino would probably be the copilot for the flight into New Brunswick.

Jaworski felt he should try to warn him.

Pinguino was fun to be around. He could laugh at himself and had the honesty of someone who freely admits wrongdoing, then goes on doing it.

"Pinguino had a gorgeous wife and two beautiful young daughters," Jaworski said. "Just beautiful children. But he always had a girlfriend. When he would talk about having a girl come over to that apartment where everybody hung out, it was never his wife....

"He used to keep the girlfriends for a couple months at a time, until they got too demanding. Then he got rid of them. His wife's job was to look after the children. He ran his household with authority and a lot of maturity, but he was immature as hell with the girlfriends. One time, when he dropped me off at the airport, Pinguino and a girlfriend were holding hands and they were all over each other like a cheap suit, you know? It was like what you would expect from high school kids in love. She lasted about a month....

"His parents were really, really traditional Colombians. They knew he was in the Mafia, but they were very, very careful not to get involved in his business. He would talk about how he was in Peru and everything. They knew what he was there for. But they were just proud of him because he had a semi-professional job and he was doing something technical. They loved their children and that was it."

When Jaworski mentioned the January 24 F-15 chase to Pinguino, "his eyes widened and I could see the fear that he had felt. He described in detail how the plane had approached them. Now that he was safely back in Colombia, he was trying to laugh about it."

As they drove through Medellin to Pinguino's condo,

Pinguino explained his financial situation. He planned to spend $70,000 to purchase his condo outright. He had already bought his parents a new home and sponsored his younger brother's flying lessons, so that he, too, could support himself flying cocaine. Pinguino sported a $10,000 Rolex watch, and although they rode in Pinguino's old Datsun, the Colombian proudly noted that he now also owned a Mercedes.

Jaworski told Pinguino that if he invested his $450,000 in Panama or Switzerland, he could make $45,000 a year without touching the principal. That would make him a wealthy man in Colombia, easily able to retire in his early twenties and support his wife and young daughters in comfort.

But Pinguino wanted more, much, much more. He had invested money in a scheme to smuggle luxury cars into the country and then resell them. Crooked diplomats could bring the cars in and dodge paying heavy customs duty. That scheme might further distance him from his country's brutal poverty.

Pinguino had been approached about working for the rival cartel based in Cali. Its leaders were generally considered of higher class than the largely blue-collar bunch in the Medellin cartel. But for all their breeding, they were second in power in the dope business. Florida newspapers had written much about a supposed war between the cartels in the summer of 1988, but Caycedo had downplayed this in conversations with Jaworski, saying that both sides went about their own business. There were enough addicts and untapped markets for everyone. Despite the overtures from Cali, Pinguino seemed happy where he was.

Pinguino noted that Pablo Escobar himself had good things to say about Jaworski's work. By cartel standards, Jaworski seemed extremely honest, since he had not been caught swindling them out of a penny. The irony was not lost on the young Canadian, nor the danger to his happy and vulnerable friend.

"Maybe it's time for you to retire," Jaworski said, knowing

that if Pinguino ventured into Canada again, he might not get back out until he had served years in prison.

Pinguino declined, saying he felt safe on any project set up by his old pal Doug Jaworski.

Jaworski kept quiet, having decided that if Pinguino didn't have enough sense to quit while he was ahead, "then maybe that's just the way it's gonna be."

Caycedo did not think he would have to murder his associate. As they chatted that afternoon in his apartment, the drug baron told Jaworski about tensions with a Miami worker named Raoul. Raoul was a mysterious figure, confined to a wheelchair and possessing a mind like a calculator. It was Raoul who organized the Montreal-area landing strips and ground personnel. Now he and Caycedo were at odds but Caycedo did not think Raoul would ever dare to split from him entirely. If he did, Raoul was a dead man.

Raoul had two superiors in Montreal who had direct access to Pablo Escobar and had known Escobar for more than a decade. The Montrealers had been trucking cocaine into Montreal from New York and were excited at the prospect of narcotics landing on their doorstep. The cartel already had airstrips near Houston, Miami, and New York and planned to buy one in Chicago. Their intention was to bring in three or four flights of 600 kilos each into New Brunswick. Big plans — and money — hinged on Jaworski's operation.

Out came more maps. The future looked bright as Caycedo talked about how they could fly from Colombia to Mexico, refuel, then continue up the western coast into British Columbia. Caycedo hoped to buy airstrips in Montana and British Columbia to service the western market, and he already had someone like Jaworski working on the project. If Jaworski came on board there, he would introduce the two, Caycedo said, declining to name his western technician. There was no need to give away such details.

This western plan was, in large part, a backup in case the eastern Canadian plans didn't work out. Both schemes were alternatives to the current system, which involved stockpiling cocaine in Mexico, then trucking it across the border to the Houston area. There it was stockpiled again, then distributed, often by motor homes. Again, Caycedo was evasive on details, steering the conversation to the confiscated JetStar, which had cost the cartel more than $500,000 and had yet to earn a penny. Caycedo explained that the executive jet would be useful for flights into an unnamed major tourist center in Mexico near Acapulco, where the chief of police was totally on the cartel payroll. There, they could load the jet and, if Jaworski was agreeable, use it to step up their penetration of European markets, including Italy, France, and London. If the cartel was to keep growing, this was the key market for expansion. Oversupply was constantly deflating North American prices.

Just then a man with a briefcase arrived at Caycedo's apartment and everything changed. The man told Caycedo that Brazilian police had beaten some of his workers during interrogation and had forced them to sign confessions.

Caycedo was livid. For the rest of the afternoon, there were endless phone calls on the topic. Maps and real estate documents about Wayman were everywhere, but that was on hold now, as Jaworski witnessed a dark, angry side of Caycedo that he had never seen before.

Caycedo called the cartel's Brazilian lawyers. Then he dispatched a hit squad to ferret out the culprits in the police there, then murder them. All it took was one short phone call from Caycedo, and there would be widows in another country.

On the final night of the three-day visit, Caycedo was his normal pleasant self. When Jaworski stepped into his room, he noticed the pocket Canon camera he had packed. The camera was just a prop so that he could act like a tourist at customs.

The Mounties had pushed him to try to get a picture of Caycedo. He had wanted a camera hidden in a briefcase, just like the ones you see in Miami spy shops, but was refused. There were no pictures of Caycedo in any of his safehouses. He did not even display photos of himself or his family in his home. Now, Caycedo stood in the light near the balcony, just fifteen feet away. He was in range for a good shot. Jaworski stood in the darkness, looking out at him. One snap of his finger and he could have the picture. The Mounties would love it. But could he keep the pop-up flash from going off? How could he laugh it off if it did?

"Fuck it, I don't need a picture that badly," Jaworski said to himself, putting down the camera and walking out to resume chatting with Caycedo.

15/ "GOTTA BE A BETTER WAY"

"Hey, you get that tap off your phone line."

— Douglas Jaworski jokes with cartel associate.

WHEN SONNY TALKED, HE WAS ALWAYS UPBEAT, enthusiastic, and humorous. Either Sonny never got angry, or the rail-thin, sixtyish man had himself well under control. A career criminal, it would be understandable if he had learned not to trust people around him enough to show his real emotions.

Sonny chainsmoked, and when he found something funny, he emitted a joyless smoker's laugh that was more like a cough that trailed on and on. Sonny spoke about things only when there was a need to do so and then said only as much as was necessary.

And Sonny seemed to have his own secrets, hinted at by his eyes, which were out of synch with his omnipresent smile.

Sonny's dark brown eyes had heavy black rings around them. The weary look wasn't from drugs or drinking. Jaworski never saw him with stimulants. Did the man ever sleep? What was he worried about? What or whom did he suspect?

"He always had this feeling of paranoia about him," Jaworski said. "He was always walking about like he had something on his mind. I never ever figured out what it was. You'd catch him in his thoughts."

When Jaworski returned to Canada, he knew that Sonny's dark, suspicious eyes were trained on him.

Jaworski called Albany on February 16, immediately after returning from Colombia. He had to know where Sonny was, what he was seeing, what he might be suspecting. The telephone was a way of keeping tabs on Sonny. As long as Sonny picked up the line in Albany, Jaworski knew he wasn't in New Brunswick, watching.

This time, a career criminal named Ron Whitaker answered the phone in Albany. Whitaker had been in and out of jail all his life and clearly didn't suspect he was being set up for yet another term.

> Jaworski: Ron, you scumbag.
> Whitaker: What's happenin', man?
> Jaworski: How you doin', boy?
> Whitaker: I'm doin' great, man, just standin' by, you know.
> Jaworski: Are you stayin' out of the pig pen [jail]?

When Sonny came on the line for a three-way conversation, they noted that the reception on the phone was weak. Jaworski could not resist an inside joke.

> Whitaker: All right, you're gonna have to holler because I can't hardly hear you.
> Sonny: Hello.

Jaworski: Hey, you get that tap off your line, you'd be able to hear just fine.

Sonny: (Laughing) Yeah, I know it.

They chatted about the possibilities of a flight heading into Albany, and if the runway was, in Jaworski's words, "close to makin' mud pies" and "startin' to smush." As the conversation waned, Jaworski made yet another joke for the benefit of police listening in, as he noted that Sonny and Whitaker had booked him into a nice hotel for his upcoming New York State visit.

Jaworski: Oh, you're gonna put me up at a nice place this time?

Sonny: Sure. You don't need to be in a rat hole place, do you?

Jaworski: A rat hole for a rat.

The next day, Sonny opened up a little. He said he needed all the money he could make, since his wife had cancer and required expensive treatments. Such natural crises can bankrupt mid-level criminals, who conduct their careers without benefit of medical insurance plans.

When Jaworski called him on February 21, Caycedo hinted that a flight might be heading north soon.

In his garbled half-code, "Daniel's place" was New York City, "information" was instructions regarding the Montreal money delivery, and "Peter" was Pablo Escobar.

"Last night, I was with Peter, you know, in the meeting, and he told me that Monday they were supposed to send the information up with Daniel."

After chatting about planes and phone systems, Jaworski fished for more information about the Albany plan. This time, a "vacation" was a drug flight.

Caycedo seemed to find Jaworski's curiosity interesting, even suspicious.

Caycedo: Very bad for vacation. Maybe until this weekend everything will be able to get through.

Jaworski: Well, okay. I don't wanna be involved with that, but, um....

Caycedo: But you're curious anyway?

16/ BREAKING APART

"I'm an honest fella."

— Cartel worker explains himself to Douglas Jaworski.

THE INFIGHTING WAS NOW VICIOUS. CAYCEDO'S rival Raoul was running him down, fueled by repeated accusations by Frank the gofer that Caycedo's worker Doug Jaworski was untrustworthy. It was verbal gunfire, the kind that quickly leads to the real thing.

Pilot Diego Ganuza relayed news when he called Jaworski in the Toronto-area bedroom community of Mississauga on February 22. Ganuza was in Miami and was being sent north to drop off "papers" — the $430,000 Caycedo had agreed to pay Jaworski.

Ganuza said he would be in Montreal the next day and would leave a message on Jaworski's answering machine. If there was any confusion, Jaworski was to call "Joseph" in Queens, New York.

Then Ganuza told how he hated it when higher-ups like Caycedo and Raoul feuded. "It's a big, big mess," Ganuza said. "And the thing is, I will have to fucking choose sides. You know, I'm stuck between a rock and a hard place."

It took murderous billionaire Pablo Escobar himself to step in and approve funding for the Canadian Maritime operation. The sting still seemed to be moving ahead.

"In front of me they approve funds for you guys," Ganuza said.

"Yeah?"

"The Pope did so....You know I've seen it."

Later that day, Caycedo called. He and Ganuza were not on good terms or exchanging information with each other. Things were even more secretive now in the cartel. Caycedo provided independent confirmation of what Ganuza had said: Caycedo had put his own neck out for Jaworski. Frank the gofer was saying that Jaworski could not be trusted. Raoul was saying the same thing. Escobar had been cautioned that Jaworski's Internal Revenue Service problems in Florida made him a bad risk. Caycedo had stuck his reputation — and quite possibly his life — behind the young Canadian's honor.

Caycedo referred to Escobar by his nickname Peter, saying, "He [Raoul] was telling Peter that he didn't want to get involved with giving you money because you have a problem."

"They're trying to make you look bad or what?" Jaworski asked.

"Well, yes, more or less," Caycedo answered. "They tried to make me look bad through you."

Caycedo noted that Jaworski had handled close to $3.5 million (U.S.) from the cartel in aircraft business. Frank the gofer, who was smearing Jaworski's reputation, was small fry by comparison. Clearly Frank the gofer had meant it when he threatened Jaworski with revenge. The Maritime operation would be his chance.

When the RCMP first saw Diego Ganuza, he was wearing his usual easygoing expression, standing a head above the rest of the crowd.

"He's as big as I am," said Corporal Milner.

Ganuza was with Jaworski in the dark of a Dorval airport office, filing toward the Customs gate. The Mounties had turned out the room lights, so that they could see out but no one could see in.

The Mounties had checked airline computers for Ganuza's arrival time from Miami. His name was found, even though Ganuza had deliberately misspelled it.

Two months after Jaworski first approached the Mounties, they got their first close-up look at their prey.

"When it comes time to bust this guy, I want to do it," Milner said.

Criminals often make a big show of hugging each other when they meet. Ostensibly it's a show of affection, but it's also a good way to check for body-pack microphones. Jaworski was wearing one on February 24, when he headed down to Ganuza's room at the Pointe-Claire Holiday Inn to pick up the $430,000 from Caycedo. The Mounties had not had the time or opportunity to bug the room, and Jaworski was edgy. Ganuza was a friendly guy and also a big, powerful ex-Marine. If he hugged Jaworski and discovered a body pack, the smile would quickly leave his face.

But he didn't. Maybe he trusted Jaworski. Maybe he just wasn't feeling that affectionate.

When Jaworski returned to his Mountie handlers that afternoon, he was beaming. Inside an ordinary-looking vinyl gym bag was $430,000. It was supposed to pay for his expenses, the New Brunswick airstrip, and back debts. "He was proud as punch," Sergeant Wayne Umansky later said.

Sergeant Umansky and Corporal Keith Milner carried the money to the Toronto-bound plane. They were "smiling like I had never seen them smile before — the corners of their mouths were going to fall into their ears," Jaworski said later. Jaworski had wanted to carry the money through airport security himself. Umansky said no. Something about having to run it under a laser for fingerprints.

Jaworski did not understand why the Mounties would not let him hold the money once he turned it over to them. Wasn't he the one who gave it to them in the first place? But the officers needed to be able to say, in court and under oath, that they had had sole possession of the money after Jaworski handed it to them. It's called continuity of evidence and is essential in preparing a court case. The sting would be a failure unless they got convictions in court. Like Caycedo, the Mounties knew that large operations turned on tiny details.

But Jaworski was hurt. "It dawned on me — an informant's an informant and that's the way it's always going to be."

On February 28, Jaworski was on the phone to Caycedo, who, as usual, displayed a career criminal's wariness of everything that could go wrong. He urged the young Canadian to find a safe spot to hide the cocaine shipment once it landed, "because nowadays there're so many robbers, you know, you get mugged or —"

Jaworski burst out laughing before Caycedo could say the word "something."

"Get mugged?"

"Yeah," Caycedo replied, but now he was laughing too.

"Get mugged? The only thing that's gonna mug me out there, pal, is a moose."

Jaworski agreed to help move the cocaine once the plane had landed, which would have earned him another $500,000. No clue was offered about whether the shipment was going to Montreal, Toronto, or New York.

The next day, Jaworski called Sonny again in Albany. By picking up the phone, Sonny answered Jaworski's first question. Sonny was still in Albany and not spying on the New Brunswick operation. The last thing they needed was Sonny or one of his men showing up unannounced in Fredericton.

Sonny and Jaworski joked about how they had used phony business cards, saying they worked for travel agencies to get cheap rates and preferential treatment from hotels while traveling.

"What'd you say my name is one day? Sunshine Tours or something?" Sonny said.

They both broke up laughing. Jaworski finally replied, "No, Snow Tours."

"Snow Tours," Sonny echoed, appreciating the pun. ("Snow" is street slang for cocaine).

Sonny stressed again how startlingly honest he had found Canadians during a recent trip north. Sonny was surprised more by honesty than by deception. He explained that it jolted him to be instantly trusted at a New Brunswick hotel.

"So the guy asked me, he says, 'You wanna pay for it now or when you check out tomorrow?' I said, 'Well, I don't know. What do you want me to do?' And he said, 'It doesn't make any difference.' I said, 'Okay, I'll just pay for it in the morning.'"

"But you did."

"I paid for it the next morning."

"Well, there you go."

"Ah, but I'm an honest fella."

That was enough to make them both break up laughing. Sonny was somehow touched by the experience, continuing, "I was impressed with that. I haven't seen that in so many years. I don't know if I've ever seen that."

Meanwhile, Sergeant Bob Lowe, the Silver Fox of the Mounties, was doing his laundry in the bathroom sink in his Albany hotel room. He was part of a team staking out the cartel's new airstrip there and the waiting had gone on far longer than anyone had expected. Sonny was ready to go, and now bad weather was all that separated authorities from a huge cocaine seizure and major arrests. Now, Mounties, as well as officials from U.S. Customs, state police, and the Drug Enforcement Administration, were all waiting and hoping that snow would lift across the eastern seaboard so that the drugs could come north. If Lowe had known it would drag on so long, he would have packed more clothes.

Some of the team couldn't help but wonder about Jaworski: Wouldn't it be just like a criminal to get everybody looking at Albany, then sneak a flight in somewhere else? Were they perhaps trusting him too much?

"This isn't going. This is bullshit," American officers grumbled.

Sergeant Bob Lowe noticed that such comments stung Jaworski, who was now shuffling between Toronto, Albany, and the Maritimes in his work with the Mounties. "I think he felt that people were blaming him for it not happening but that was not the case. He had done everything he was asked to do to make that a success."

Sergeant Lowe sat for days on end in his hotel room in Albany, watching the all-weather cable network for an indication of when the weather would clear up. Jaworski had told him that Caycedo had the same viewing habits, and Lowe found it ironic to think that, down in Colombia — on the opposite side of the law and the shipment — an adversary he had never seen was watching the same television program and wishing for exactly the same thing.

"Fuck you guys!" Jaworski shouted. "I'll go work for somebody else!"

The explosion was two weeks in the making. It was that long since Jaworski had delivered the $430,000 to the Mounties, and the tensions had finally come to a boil. He considered $180,000 of the $430,000 his, payment for past debts from Caycedo.

He kept nagging, and the Mounties repeatedly told him to stop worrying. No one seemed to trust Jaworski and everyone wanted to control him. It wasn't fun any more. Then he exploded.

"My attitude was 'What am I doing this for?'" Jaworski later said. "I must be right out of my mind to be working this hard. I'm away from my home. I'm away from my wife. It's causing my marriage to blow up and these guys are telling me that I can't have the money that this guy owes me. I couldn't understand it, since I went to all the trouble to get the money in Montreal instead of Panama. I felt like I was getting shafted."

Doug Jaworski, informer and cartel associate, was righteous. "I gave them a quarter of a million dollars for doing absolutely nothing. But they wanted $430,000 for doing absolutely nothing. Just because they have got the badge. And I was really kind of disgusted."

Suddenly, what promised to be the biggest drug sting in Canadian history was in tatters. The star informer, the Mounties' sole link to the top level of the cartel, had just quit.

17/ SOREL REVISITED

"You know, I'm always retiring. I'm always thinkin'
of that."

— Diego Caycedo to Douglas Jaworski.

THE COMPUTER PROGRAMMER WANTED TO
know what the young man who was sharing the ski lift did for
a living.

"I'm a pilot," answered Doug Jaworski, truthfully adding
that he was unemployed at the moment.

The scenario was repeated throughout the afternoon as
Jaworski skied the hills of Collingwood, near Toronto.

Then, when he got back into his car at the end of the day,
Jaworski checked the answering machine on his cellular phone
for messages.

More than two dozen had been left by the Mounties.

About halfway through the messages was an important
change in tone. He would get the $180,000.

It was all Jaworski needed to hear to transform him again

from Mountie defector to undercover agent. The sting was reborn.

Jaworski flew down to New York State, where his old friend Pinguino was happy to see him. Pinguino had been sent north to conduct a cartel version of a quality-control inspection and critique the airstrip near Fredericton. He wore a beautiful, buttery-soft new black leather jacket when he met Jaworski on March 2. The jacket was meant as a gift for Jaworski. But Pinguino had not anticipated the cold, and so he joked that he needed to wear it for the drive before giving it to his friend. The jacket was repayment for a gift Jaworski had bought Pinguino during a trip to Texas the previous summer. "When he heard I was going to Texas, he went wild for a pair of genuine American cowboy boots. They watch all the American movies in South America. The funny thing was that he could buy better quality cowboy boots in Colombia for maybe a tenth of the price. While I was out there, I bought him some gray, eelskin cowboy boots. When he got them, he really went nuts. He really liked them. These were genuine from Texas — right from Texas."

Pinguino had ignored Jaworski's subtle warning down in Colombia. Now he was cheerful that he would be flying north again, right into a trap set by someone he considered a close friend.

Jaworski felt obliged to try again to warn him.

"Are you going to be involved in this for a career or not?" Jaworski asked him.

"Man, we're in the Mafia," Pinguino said, proudly. "This is the Mafia."

"Fuck, we're going to have problems if we start doing this too much," Jaworski said. "Look, you do one trip and we'll talk later and see if it's safe."

There was a strong possibility the RCMP was going to let the first plane into New Brunswick return to Colombia. Arrests would be made after the second flight, giving the Mounties more time and a deeper look at the cartel's Canadian operations. That should mean more arrests, more convictions, more damage. Maybe Pinguino could sneak through and make another $150,000. He would never know how lucky he was.

"I know Diego's pushing me to become cocaine central as soon as it works once and I might not want to do this any more," Jaworski continued. "You do this once and I'll tell you how it goes. Make sure you communicate with me before you do another."

"I don't want to fly to Sorel any more," Pinguino said. He had tried not to show it around other cartel pilots, but the January chase by the American F-15 fighter plane had left him badly shaken. Pinguino was close to his family and the thought of being arrested and imprisoned in a foreign country would give anyone a scare.

"I only want to do a deal that you're involved in," Pinguino said.

Sneaking Pinguino into New Brunswick meant traveling back roads that had been frequented by bootleggers in the time of Prohibition. Undercover Mounties Keith Milner and Wayne Umansky were trailing them in a rental car, along with a DEA agent in a four-wheel drive. The RCMP had already notified Canadian Customs that they would be, in effect, smuggling an illegal alien into the country.

Jaworski was at the wheel as he and Pinguino drove north along Interstate I-95 north toward Houlton, Maine. Pinguino was a small man — not too much bigger than a jockey — and not a threatening person, although he sometimes acted like a cowboy and packed a gun in a shoulder holster. Pinguino chatted easily as they drove, telling Jaworski, among other things, that the pilot Diego Ganuza was now in Colombia.

Jaworski had been driving his Chevrolet Baretta at seventy miles an hour, but he now sped to eighty-five. Its ride was smooth and Pinguino did not pay any attention to the speed. But behind them, the DEA agent in the four-wheel drive cursed into his radio to Milner and Umansky. Had Jaworski gone nuts? What was the point of the impromptu stock car race? Jaworski knew the DEA agent's four-wheel drive had a nasty rattle once it broke sixty. At eighty-five miles an hour, it would be like riding a jackhammer.

Jaworski kept his foot hard on the pedal.

Finally, he wheeled into a Pizza Hut and the Mounties discreetly pulled up behind them. Jaworski knew they would want to tell him to smarten up and slow down. Corporal Milner tried to lay on a New England accent as he ordered a pizza to go, then followed Jaworski into the washroom. From an adjoining urinal, Milner gave Jaworski a pithy assessment of his driving abilities.

"Slow the fuck down!" Milner commanded.

"Are you finished?" Jaworski replied, smiling. Then he continued, "Get surveillance on Sorel. There's going to be a flight into Sorel."

The high speed had been a stunt to force the Mounties to confront Jaworski. Otherwise, they would have hung back and out of sight and he would not have been able to tip them off.

Since Pinguino had told him that Ganuza was down in Colombia, Jaworski reasoned the cartel must be getting ready for another flight to Sorel. This would be perfect. The sting would wind up quickly and Pinguino would not go to jail. Jaworski's role might also remain a secret. Since he was not directly involved in the Sorel operation, Caycedo might not suspect him. And Pinguino would still consider Jaworski a friend, never even hearing about his friend's betrayal.

Jaworski found the washroom scene with Milner strangely symbolic and amusing, considering the high-stakes game they were playing. "There we were, with our dicks in our hands, discussing my life — my future — and the RCMP mandate for the next few months," Jaworski later said.

Further down the road, the Mounties met up with a DEA surveillance team, then crossed into Canada at Woodstock, New Brunswick. As planned, everyone headed to the Howard Johnson motor lodge in Fredericton, where Jaworski had agreed in advance to meet. Pinguino was tired, and when he dozed off, Jaworski snuck over to the Mounties' room and gave them a rundown of what he had heard on the drive up. Milner was now combing his hair differently, so that if Pinguino noticed him in both locales, he might not realize it was the same person. It was a little detail, but perhaps an important one. Jaworski didn't even notice the change.

The next day, Jaworski and Pinguino surveyed tiny Wayman Field from the air. Wayman Field was a small private airstrip that belonged to a retired couple who were out of the country, but who had enthusiastically agreed to cooperate with the Mounties. The airstrip was near auto routes heading south, but also out of the way, making it a prime spot for Caycedo's operations. Up until the hatching of the drug scheme, the largest industry in the area was a chick hatchery in nearby Burtt's Corner, followed by an egg business.

Later on March 3, Jaworski and Pinguino were driving back to New England. Milner and Umansky became separated from them and decided to take a shortcut to catch up, racing their Pontiac Grand Am through tiny villages before stopping at a McDonald's near Bangor. The girl who served them looked about seventeen and was just about to get off work. After giving them their order, she headed out the door, saying, "Good night, fellas." Then she paused, turned around, and floored the undercover Mounties by joking, "What are you guys doing in Lincoln, Maine? What are you? A couple of dope dealers?" It was a totally off-the-wall statement, meant as nothing more than an innocent joke. The Mounties, light-headed from too little sleep and too much adrenalin, turned to each other and broke into laughter.

Down in Medellin, Caycedo was also giddy. Like the Mounties, the drug baron finally felt that all his efforts to control Doug Jaworski were about to pay off.

Now, on March 8, Caycedo wanted to check final details about the New Brunswick airstrip. It had passed Pinguino's inspection with ease. All Caycedo needed were answers to a few questions. Was the airstrip firm enough for a plane to land safely or had winter thaw made it muddy? And could Jaworski have some 300 feet of trees at the end of the runway trimmed? Caycedo had to have long, easy runs in and out of airstrips for his pilots and their expensive cargo. They would be tired when they arrived, and there was no point risking an accident. The Mounties, however, could not start trimming trees without the permission of the airstrip's real owners. Jaworski told Caycedo that he could guarantee a safe landing, and that he did not want to waste time chopping down trees.

Caycedo's eagerness to begin the operation made him vulnerable to Jaworski's argument. So did his sense of humor. Caycedo had earlier been convulsed with laughter when Jaworski reported the weather up in Canada was "hotter than a queer at a wienie roast." The drug baron had laughed harder still when Jaworski complained that his love life was so bad he "couldn't get laid in a women's prison with a pocketful of pardons."

> Caycedo: Is it [the runway] nice and firm?
> Jaworski: (Laughing) As firm as you like it?
> Caycedo: Is it hard, I mean?

Jaworski: You're getting to be a dirty old man.

Caycedo: No, no, no. I mean it. I mean it. (Laughing) I'm serious when I say that. Is it nice and hard? I mean for Jay's [pilot Jose Ali Galindo-Escobar] use?

Jaworski: Yes.

Caycedo: Okay.

Jaworski: Just the way he likes it.

Caycedo: All right. Listen, eh? Fernando [Pinguino] was telling me that he recommended cutting down those expenses [trees]. Remember, he told you?

Jaworski: Well, you're gonna get about five days' delay if you want me to do that.

Caycedo: Oh, don't say that. Do me a favor. At least start tomorrow, cutting down as much as you can. Remember, Jay cannot take any chances.

Caycedo was clearly happy now. He seemed to have ridden out the threats from Raoul and Frank the gofer. Apparently, Caycedo did not even know that Frank the gofer would soon be working in Canada for Raoul. Caycedo made it clear that there would be plenty of work for Jaworski in the future.

Jaworski: Well, you know I'm not a careerist. I'm not gonna be in this forever.

Caycedo: So am I. You know, I'm always retiring. I'm always thinking of that. (Laughs) But with banks and mortgage payments and those things, you know we're interested in seeing that money. Then, how do you like my proposal?

Jaworski: I'll give it a shot.

There was still one complication, but not a major one, in Caycedo's opinion. He was getting married the next day. Caycedo told Jaworski to call him at five the next afternoon, so that he could get to the wedding on time. Neither one was overly sentimental about the occasion.

Jaworski: She got big tits, or what?

Caycedo: You know her.

Jaworski: Who?

Caycedo: You know my wife. (Laughs) I wasn't married, you know. I'm just getting married.

Jaworski: Oh my God.

Caycedo: I have to be there at six-thirty. That's why I am asking you to call me at five. So I have time to go and get dressed.

The next day, forty-five minutes before Caycedo's scheduled nuptials, he and Jaworski haggled about money over the telephone. Jaworski wanted an advance to pay his ground crew. Caycedo explained that this just was not how things were done in the cartel. Jaworski knew this but, as usual, expected some kind of special accommodation. In the cartel, drugs were delivered first, then the crews were paid. Even his good feelings about Jaworski, the deal, and the wedding did not change this, since it would mean introducing Jaworski to people he was not supposed to know. It was one thing to laugh at Jaworski's crude jokes, but quite another to compromise business operations.

If Caycedo had a honeymoon, it was measured in hours and not days. The day after his wedding, on March 10, 1989, Jaworski and Caycedo spoke between Burtt's Corner and Medellin. Caycedo seemed anxious but confident. The Mounties were also anxious. Finally, for a brief moment, Jaworski, Caycedo, and the Mounties all thought they had things under control.

18/ RUDE AWAKENING

"Nobody knows who's doing what out there."

— Douglas Jaworski as the sting gets complicated.

JAWORSKI WAS AWAKENED AT 3 A.M. BY A SHARP knock on his Fredericton hotel door. Jaworski let Sergeant Bob Lowe in, then groggily slid back into bed.

"We just caught Ganuza in Sorel," the Mountie said.

"Great," Jaworski replied.

Everyone should be happy now. Jaworski could quickly fulfill his commitment to the Mounties, shuck the tax charges and threat of jail, and maybe even patch up his marriage. Caycedo would probably believe him and not press the issue if Jaworski said the Sorel bust had unnerved him. And since Jaworski's friend Pinguino wasn't scheduled to fly into Sorel, he would also be safe.

In the meantime, perhaps Jaworski could even get back to sleep.

Thirty seconds later Sergeant Lowe still had not said anything more. He also had not left the room. Jaworski looked up at him and met the Silver Fox interrogator's stare.

"Why are you looking at me?" Jaworski finally asked.

"The dope got away."

That was the worst thing that could have happened. Now Caycedo would put the Maritime operation on hold indefinitely as he evaluated what went wrong. Maybe Jaworski's duplicity would be discovered. Maybe Caycedo would shift his attentions toward a safer location and ruin hopes of a sting. There was no way of knowing what Caycedo would do now.

"What happened to the surveillance at Sorel?"

"There wasn't any."

"Why not?"

"I don't know."

Sergeant Lowe went on to say that someone in U.S. Customs suggested that perhaps Jaworski had been duping the Mounties, getting them to focus their energies on New Brunswick to divert attention from Sorel.

"Bob, I told you to put surveillance on Sorel. I never told you to take it off."

It would have been the biggest narcotics bust in Canada's history, something to make up for all the late nights, the encounters with scummy drug dealers, and the near misses that are a drug cop's lot. Law makers and future police officers wishing to know how the cartel works in North America would have studied its every nuance, and they would all have been impressed by the precision, teamwork, and improvising skills of the Mounties working on it. Criminals would also study it to see how to become better law breakers. Instead, it was a screw-up. The less said the better.

The Commander 980 executive turbojet had been flown by Diego Ganuza, the same pilot who had handed Jaworski $430,000 in downtown Montreal three weeks before. The flight into Sorel, about sixty miles northeast of Montreal, had gone up from South America through what had been dubbed the "New York Express" during marijuana runs of the 1970s. It kept on going, outside the American "electronic fence" of radar networks.

Ganuza had been chased, just as he had in January. The potential huge drug seizure first appeared as a minute blip on the screen of an Airborne Warning and Control System (AWACS), the computerized radar system of a U.S. Air Force jet on a training mission over southern Florida. The AWACS system had been developed to help coordinate air battles, but was being used for drug interdiction after the U.S. Congress set aside $300 million in the fall of 1988 for the American military to catch drug planes. The U.S. military had previously resisted such work because it did not want to expose its members to bribes and other corrupting influences, but the crush of drugs on the street forced the government to increase surveillance.

The North American Air Defence Command (NORAD) dispatched two F-16 fighter jets from Maine to track the Commander, and their crews noted it did not have running lights or a flight plan and was heading in the direction of Nova Scotia. When the fighter jets ran low on fuel, they handed over the surveillance to another pair of F-16s, whose pilots tried to hang far enough back to keep from being detected. Since the military's new powers in the U.S. drug fight gave it authority to follow planes, but not to stop or arrest their pilots, they then had to hand the case over to the U.S. Customs Service interdiction unit.

Luckily, because of the Jaworski case, there was a turbojet and a Blackhawk helicopter waiting in Bangor, Maine. The jet took off immediately, while the Blackhawk crew looked for Mounties who had been working with them that day in

Bangor so that they would be able to make an arrest inside Canada.

Ganuza was experienced at this now. He began flying a slow, meandering course, floating back and forth between the Canadian and American borders. By flying deliberately slowly, he put the faster jets in constant danger of overshooting him. But Ganuza did not have much fuel to play with in the late stages of his 3,000-mile flight.

The Blackhawk crew could not contact the Mounties. Apparently, someone had forgotten to put an office phone on call forward and the call was missed. It was such a tiny detail but also a crucial one, the type that the Mounties and Caycedo struggled to control. The type that makes people on both sides of the drug wars paranoid.

Finally, the Blackhawk took off in pursuit of the Commander. By 11 p.m., the Commander was approaching Sorel. If the landing was in American territory, the Blackhawk crew would land alongside the Commander, seize the drugs, and arrest its crew.

But since the Commander touched down in Sorel, the American was forced to circle in the air, waiting for either permission from Canada to land or the arrival of Canadian authorities to make an arrest. Meanwhile, the Blackhawk raced to catch up.

On the ground, a small truck approached the landed Commander. Through night-vision goggles, the Americans watched helplessly as the Commander crew scurried to unload duffel bags into the truck.

The Americans circled for ten minutes before finally getting permission to land. As they did so, the loaded truck was driven away. Left on the runway was the empty Commander, with a registration number painted over and replaced with a makeshift Canadian flag. The frustrated customs officers forced the pilot

Ganuza, his copilot, and the airport manager to lie face down on the ground, bloodying the manager's nose in the process.

Finally, police pulled up. In a fitting ending to the fiasco, police bickered about who was in charge as the truck sped away into the dark with a suspected 500 kilos of cocaine.

Ganuza and his copilot could be charged only with minor infractions, such as bringing a stolen plane into Canada, and were able to pay their $23,000 fines in cash before being deported. As Ganuza avoided jail, Canadian authorities further embarrassed themselves by filing a diplomatic protest to the United States the next day for possible "violation of Canadian sovereignty." Once Ottawa caught on to the full picture, the protest was quietly withdrawn. Understandably, no one in power wanted to call further public attention to the bungling.

For Canadian and American authorities, the case was a humbling reminder of the need to streamline military and police bureaucracies. What could have been a great arrest was replaced by finger-pointing and suspicion.

It was back to sitting around hotel rooms and waiting for Jaworski and the Mounties. The whole thing was beginning to remind Jaworski of day-to-day life with the cartel. In effect, he was still playing the same game, just with a different side. Cops and criminals both seemed to thrive on adrenalin and kept score by adding up how much money and drugs they had at the end of the day. Street-level police and cartel workers both took orders from unseen entities, living in Ottawa and Medellin respectively. "With both groups, it's hanging around in hotel rooms and safehouses," Jaworski said. "Everybody has a gun. Everybody just hangs around, waiting for something to happen.... But down in Colombia, at least they get the girls to come out and have a big party."

Eating habits also differed markedly. "With the Colombians, it was a fight to see who would get to pay for a round of drinks. With the Mounties, everybody disappeared when the bill came around. The Mounties didn't want to go over their [$40] per diem and they wanted to make money off the fucking thing, so they ate the shittiest food you can imagine. It was ridiculous. I gained twenty pounds on that case because of all the crap that we were eating. The classic line I ever heard from one of them is that Wendy's is too expensive."

Now, there was plenty of time for waiting and hoping, for being one of the guys. Caycedo and Escobar were studying the Sorel interception and everything was on hold. On March 14, Caycedo said that Pablo Escobar should have it all figured out within three days. But on March 20, all Caycedo would say was that Escobar was still investigating.

Jaworski had trouble sitting still. Maybe it was time for a quick visit to Florida. When he flew south, he found things grim there as well. Susan had two friends over; one was in the midst of a divorce, the other was breaking up with her boyfriend. The unhappy threesome went out and Jaworski stayed home and called Sergeant Bob Lowe in Toronto and pressed for details of what went wrong at Sorel. Sergeant Lowe said he could not give answers yet.

"In other words, there's a good chance they already blew the cookie basket," Jaworski said, his words code for "There's a good chance the cartel knows about the sting."

"Oh, I don't think so," Lowe replied. "I've got nothing to judge that on. Nothing at all. I really don't know."

Jaworski said it was strange that, in a recent conversation, Caycedo said that he should call back in the next ten days. Usually, the Colombian kept his workers on a far tighter rein.

Jaworski wanted to know exactly what happened to the pilot and copilot who were captured at Sorel. What did they say? What were they told? His mood worsened when he was told they were deported from Canada.

"How's the booty doing?" Jaworski asked, referring to the cargo of cocaine.

"Oh, we're working on it," Lowe replied. "We can't move too quick."

"I've heard evasive answers before, but you're the best."

Lowe didn't sound bothered by the dig, continuing, "Well, you just can't jump into these things. You've got to wait for some rats to come to the cheese. You know what I mean?"

Was word out on Jaworski's role in the sting? This was the second time that a cartel plane had been chased en route to Sorel. They must suspect something.

"I just wish I knew what they [the cartel] were doing...," Jaworski said. "So now that he [the Colombian copilot] is out, I'm sure he's going to be on the phone. If they blew the cookie jar, I had better be watching out real close. Here's the thing, if they did, and he got deported, then I've already got a problem. Right now. And I'm sitting here thinking life is just fucking wonderful. And there could very well be, already, a big problem for me and my parents."

"What do you think if you phoned down again?" Sergeant Lowe asked.

"I'm not hesitant to do that but I would really like to know what the hell they [the pilot and copilot at Sorel] said before I do that. We've got a bunch of other problems that we have to deal with right away. My dad is just freaking out. I sent him a fax. Because it involves him so much, I have to tell him. You know?"

"What did you tell him?" Lowe asked.

"I just told him about as much as he needs to know. I told him that there was bad news."

"What did he say?"

"Well, he was more concerned about the fact that he's established and he's in business," Jaworski replied. "If he can't sell it in time, what's going to happen with that? My dad's pretty concerned about that. I said that the organization [RCMP] would take care of it, but that was a pretty broad statement on my part."

The issue of the safety of Jaworski's parents posed enormous potential complications to the case. Lowe said he did not think the lives of Jaworski or his parents were in danger because of the Sorel foul-up.

"That could be wishful thinking," Jaworski replied. "That's one thing that I've learned. Nobody knows who's doing what out there."

"Some people do."

"Yeah. But some people know most of it but nobody knows all of it," Jaworski said.

What Sergeant Lowe didn't know was that Jaworski was now secretly taping his telephone calls with the Mounties. Taped evidence was obviously valuable to the police as a method of managing informers like Jaworski. Maybe he could gain some control over his destiny by doing the same thing. "It could possibly have been a tool in the future in case the RCMP decided to renege on any of its commitments," he later said.

He also secretly taped telephone fights with Susan, then replayed them late at night. He couldn't figure out what was going wrong in his marriage either, or how to control it.

19/ CRASH

"You'll like it, you little devil."

— Diego Caycedo to Douglas Jaworski.

"HE CALLED ME," CAYCEDO SAID ON THE LONG-distance line between Medellin and Fredericton on April 2. "He said that he checked his baggage and he's going by the way, with his wife and the three kids. That's five. Five of them."

The code was easy to decipher and delightful. Jaworski laughed as he heard it, knowing instantly that "five of them" meant 500 kilos of cocaine, worth about $250 million on the streets.

"Okay," Jaworski said.

Caycedo laughed too, then added, "You'll like it, you little devil."

The sting was under way.

Later that night Doug Jaworski showed up, in a panic, at RCMP headquarters in Fredericton to see Inspector Wayne

Blackburn. Jaworski's handlers could no longer keep him calm. It was eight hours until the cocaine touched down, and Jaworski was out of control.

He demanded guarantees that his parents would be absolutely safe after the sting. Was it a scam? Or the terror of a child who thinks he may have killed the only people who really love and trust him? Throughout the operation, Blackburn had gone to great pains to ensure that no bystanders would be placed at risk by the sting. Now he was being asked to protect people he had never met who lived in the British Virgin Islands, just two hours by air from Pablo Escobar. If not, Jaworski, the central player in the sting, would quit once again. Blackburn later recalled, "We were at the point where there was no way we could stop or turn around. It was like being halfway down a slide."

Jaworski told Blackburn that he had taken Frank the gofer to meet his parents. Now Jaworski said he was terrified they would be in danger if the cartel learned of his role in the sting. For the first time in the case, Jaworski totally stunned Blackburn. Frank the gofer had personally threatened revenge against Jaworski for cutting him out of aircraft dealings with Caycedo. His superiors in the Medellin cartel were infamous for savoring bloody vengeance. And someone as intelligent as Jaworski invited them over to meet his parents one Christmas?

Jaworski's critics in the force would later say that he was strategically releasing information for his own gain. In this view, Jaworski hadn't been stupid at all. It was an enormously clever move, a way of scamming some money for his parents by forcing the Mounties to buy their business and relocate them. According to this argument, Jaworski wasn't crying for help but trying to extort from the Mounties.

Jaworski would later argue that he continually told his Mountie handlers about his fear for his parents and pointed to the taped March 21 telephone conversation with Sergeant

Bob Lowe as proof. "I mentioned it through the whole case and they kept patting me on the hand, saying, 'Don't worry about it.'"

In their early morning meeting at the Fredericton police station, Blackburn said there were limits to what an inspector like him could do. He did not have the power to promise anything concrete about money or relocation. That was Ottawa's job. "But actually allowing people to be imperiled and be in danger — we would not let that happen," Blackburn added.

These seemingly innocuous words created enormous complications for Blackburn, since he was not really supposed to deal with Jaworski face to face. Mounties control informers by limiting their contacts to a small group of handlers, who in turn report to superiors like Blackburn. Now, suddenly, Jaworski had short-circuited the process. Blackburn was being asked to make promises that were outside his job description and that dealt with virgin territory for Canada and the United States. But he was also dealing with what appeared to be a terrified young man, the largest narcotics sting in Canadian history, an unbendable deadline, and the possible slaughter of innocent people. He had to make his decision instantly. Small wonder many police officers view informers with a mixture of disgust and fear.

Jaworski's plea placed Blackburn's career in jeopardy, but there were more important things at stake than careers, and Blackburn had the reputation of being a decent person as well as a solid cop. Blackburn later recalled, "The policy of the RCMP is that if we know and believe that people's safety is in danger, especially Canadian citizens', we do everything we can to get that person out of danger." Blackburn could not take refuge in precedents because there were none; no Canadian had infuriated Pablo Escobar like this before. Escobar was internationally infamous for the ruthlessness with which he handled Colombian informers and their families. Would he be any different with a family that lived just two hours from Medellin? It was clear from the tapes that Escobar was directly involved. Was this doubly thrilling, terrifying, or both for Jaworski? Was the confrontation meant to put Jaworski in control and make things exciting, just when they appeared about to die down? Wasn't this just the sort of thing a clever sociopath would find entertaining?

Definite answers to these questions could come only via a cartel hit squad.

Blackburn told Jaworski that the Mounties would send an investigator to the British Virgin Islands, and a witness protection specialist to tell his parents what had happened and what might happen. The Mounties would also start an assessment of exactly what the threat was to Jaworski's parents.

About five hours later, Jaworski was still awake, but his mood was far different. Along with a dozen Mounties, he sat in a log cabin at Wayman Field, trying to prove he knew cruder jokes than anyone in his presence. By combining gonorrhea, pyorrhea, diarrhea, and worms into one story about a honeymoon, Doug Jaworski won the contest easily. He fit in perfectly, again the chameleon.

By eight o'clock, Corporal Keith Milner was in the control tower of the Fredericton airport, sipping coffee and chatting as the day shift replaced the night crew of tower operators. A white Commander 980 with no flight plan floated in barely above tree level.

"There are our boys," Milner said.

One of the Commander's crew had happened to glance out a window over Fredericton and noticed a small plane flying in the same direction about thirty seconds behind it. The Colombians panicked and dropped down hard, not realizing the other plane was not police surveillance, only an Eye in the

Sky plane broadcasting radio traffic reports. Bad nerves were understandable at the end of a thirteen-hour nonstop flight from Colombia. Especially this one.

As it reached Wayman Air Field, undercover police officer Varouj Pogharian looked up at the Commander, turned to fellow undercover policeman Len McMaster, and said, "Len, take a good look at this. That's the mother lode. You and I will never get to see this again. Len, you don't know how long I've waited to see this."

The Mounties in New Brunswick were almost as jumpy as the airborne Colombians. Were the pilots armed? If so, would they come out shooting if the sting was exposed? Was the runway tarmac firm enough? Spring was coming on quickly, and Blackburn had worried that the gravelly tarmac might become porous and soft, meaning the plane might spin out of control when it touched down. Blackburn and others in his group had continually walked and measured the tarmac, although they could not actually do much beyond keeping it plowed of snow.

Blackburn had recently driven a truck down the tarmac, and when he braked, the truck spun sideways. Would the Commander do the same thing? Had they spent all this energy to engineer a plane crash? Jaworski had tried to reassure him by saying, "Oh, no, there's no problem there. There's reverse thrust that will stop it."

Not being an airplane expert, the inspector had to trust Jaworski.

Blackburn was a firm believer in Murphy's Law. He had even disregarded a Caycedo directive and moved 1,200 gallons of flight fuel in a truck away from the end of the airport, so that a crash would not also mean loss of life to the two dozen camouflaged police now hiding in the woods.

And what about Sonny? Was he somewhere in the area, perhaps hiding in the woods, watching the camouflaged Mounties watch for the Colombians?

Lightly, softly, horrifyingly, the Commander floated down from the sky, brushing a scrubby spruce tree. It was a gentle touch, yet it filled experienced police officers with dread.

Sergeant Bob Lowe was hiding in a shed with another officer, filming the Commander's arrival. When the plane touched the tree, Lowe felt shock. Four months of precision police work might literally go up in flames because a spruce tree was a couple of feet too high. Caycedo had not let them know where the drugs were going and the project might end in the woods of New Brunswick, in a deathly blaze.

As the Commander continued its descent, Jaworski gripped an ax, ready to chop the pilots free if the Commander crashed. He was worried the Mounties might rush out to save lives, ruining the sting. "Everybody stay calm! Everybody stay calm! It's okay," he yelled into his hand-held radio.

When the plane touched down, Jaworski realized that under stress Jay, the pilot, had done something brilliant. He hit the brakes early and the Commander spun out violently at a ninety-degree angle. The runway was effectively blocked, and no pursuit plane would have room to land behind him. Jaworski later said that it was he who had suggested this tactic to Jay.

Smoke clouds surrounded the Commander as Jay and Pinguino hopped out and ran.

"The other plane! The other plane!" Pinguino shouted, referring to the Eye in the Sky radio crew plane, which he still thought was piloted by police. The Commander appeared ready to explode as the ground crew — actually undercover police officers — rushed toward it.

The pilots sprinted toward a pickup truck, yelling at Jaworski to burn the Commander and destroy all evidence.

They could hide away in a hotel room until things calmed down, Jaworski shouted back.

In less than a minute, the pilots were being driven away in the pickup. Two undercover police officers were posing as drivers hired by Jaworski. The pilots slipped out of their jump suits and into street clothes. Pinguino had a long-barreled chrome .38 in a shoulder holster. He explained that he would have blasted the occupants of the other airplane, had it managed to land at Wayman Air Field. But he put down the gun when undercover officer Varouj Pogharian suggested the Colombians ride in the cab of the truck. As they moved, Pogharian quickly spirited away the weapon, hiding it in a toolbox.

Meanwhile, inside the Commander, the stinging smell of fumes was overwhelming, and puddles of gas were everywhere. One spark meant fiery death.

"Get back! Get back!" Jaworski shouted at Sergeant Wayne Umansky and another Mountie who were hefting gas-soaked twenty-kilo bags of cocaine off the plane.

"No, my boss wants some dope! I've got to have some dope!" they shouted back, with no time to enjoy the irony of their comments.

Jaworski hopped into the plane, climbed over fuel drums and bales of cocaine to shut off the fuel pump. Spinning the propeller cooled the overheated engines. Then Jaworski — who was smaller than the rest of the Mountie crew — climbed into the cramped baggage area and hauled out the gasoline-soaked bales of cocaine.

Suddenly he spotted something and let out a wild yell.

"Put that fucking thing out!" he screamed as a Mountie started to light a cigarette.

The cigarette was extinguished. There was no explosion. The sting could continue.

Once the pilots were long gone, about three dozen Mounties in white camouflaged snowsuits came out of the woods and posed for snapshots in front of the mother lode. Some shots picked up the fact that the Commander was marked C-FRMP; the final three letters a joke by Jaworski, which came as close as he thought safely possible to "RCMP." Whenever planes were flown in or out of Colombia, their markings were altered by what Caycedo called his team of "Picassos," resident artists whose job was to doctor aircraft markings. On the tail section of this Commander, a Picasso had left his rough version of a Canadian flag. He clearly needed more practice.

Pinguino wanted his pistol back now. They were in the City Motel and things had calmed down.

Corporal Pogharian wore a bullet-proof vest but carried no handgun. He replied that he had thrown it away because police would come down hard on them if they somehow found the weapon.

Pinguino seemed to buy that. Then Pogharian was sent out to fetch sandwiches and pop for the pilots as they awaited Jaworski. Such pampering seemed the norm for the international men in Caycedo's pool of top pilots.

By 9:10 that morning, Jaworski was in the pilots' motel room, trying to calm them down. Jay said he had no passport, since he had expected to fly the Commander back to Colombia. They were concerned about a plane that had followed them for a while in the Caribbean. Jay suspected their route had been compromised by a rival pilot as part of the bitter internal power struggle in the cartel. As Jaworski assured them that everything was all right, he made a point of telling the pilots that they were free to go. The comment may have seemed odd and out of place to the pilots, but Jaworski said it for a reason. He had been instructed to do so by the Mounties, so that the pilots could not later claim in court that they had been subjects of a de facto arrest but had not been read their rights. It seemed a tiny detail, but those were the scary ones. The sting would blow up in their faces if it was tossed out of court on a technicality.

By 10:25 a.m., Jaworski was on the phone to Colombia, telling Caycedo that things were under control.

Meanwhile, the pilots were glancing at that week's issue of *Maclean's* magazine. Coincidentally, the cover story was entitled "A Deadly Plague of Drugs: inside the grim world of assassinations, gang wars — and addicts who will kill for a fix." The article by Chris Wood described how nearly two million Canadians sought temporary refuge in illegal drugs, and detailed how the use of highly addictive crack cocaine was spreading rapidly. Since crack's recent appearance on Canadian streets, break-ins and violence had increased markedly. *Maclean's* quoted doctors who said that 75 percent of those who use crack just three times become hooked to its cycle of intense highs and overpowering lows. It ominously noted that things were even worse in American neighborhoods, where crack had a longer history. The magazine told of a mother in the Bronx who held down her six-year-old daughter while several men raped her, all so she could receive a payment of crack cocaine. The article also noted that a cartel flight was almost nabbed earlier that winter in Sorel. Pinguino studied it and grinned.

After the call, the pilots insisted on switching rooms, afraid the long-distance call would somehow be traced to them. Jay was looser now, telling how he had flown more than 10,000 kilos of cocaine into Mexico for the cartel. The loads were between 600 and 800 kilos, and Jay's payment was $100,000 a flight. His earnings had helped him buy a fertilizer plant in Colombia, he told the undercover officers. The pilots rounded out the day with naps, then steaks, a quick shopping trip at a local mall, St.-Hubert barbecued chicken, and a move to yet another motel, just in case there were police around.

The next day, April 4, 1989, the Mounties recorded a three-way phone conversation in Spanish and English between Fredericton and Colombia. On the line were Jaworski, Diego Caycedo, and Jay. Jaworski was referred to by his code name

Daniel. For this brief period of time, both the Mounties and the cartel were full of praise for Jaworski's role in the landing. The chameleon had managed to fit into two environments simultaneously.

Caycedo: And the departure was easy? Or was there lots of....
Jaworski: No problem.
Caycedo: So the airstrip was all right then?
Jay: Because of Daniel, everything's perfect.
Caycedo: That asshole is well organized.
Jay: Holy Mary, what a well-organized thing.

Caycedo and Jay did not realize that the well-organized person they were praising was actually Inspector Wayne Blackburn of the Mounties. And Blackburn's plan was far from over.

20/ CLOSING THE NET

"Have you heard from Dew-glass?"

— Cartel pilots ask about Douglas Jaworski.

THE NUMBNESS IN CORPORAL VAROUJ Pogharian's left side kept getting worse. It was his job to accompany the cartel pilots, Jay and Pinguino. Act as a host, keep them out of trouble, and set them up for arrest. The Mounties couldn't throw them in jail yet because that would tip off Caycedo and ruin the capture of his distribution squad. Initially, the RCMP had wanted to send Jay and Pinguino back for another load. This would have bought more time for police to take a deep, wide, and unprecedented look at the cartel's top Canadian operations. The more they saw, the more damage they could do. But that plan died when the Commander spun sideways into the snow ditch at Wayman Field.

Ironically, nobody had really wanted the pilots' arrest. At least, not now. Caycedo wanted the pilots to fly back home quickly on a direct flight. He promised to pay off the right people at the southern end to ensure they could quietly slip back into Colombia. But if the Mounties set Jay and Pinguino free, it would be enormously embarrassing if ever made public. So Corporal Pogharian and Corporal Len McMaster were stuck playing gracious hosts to two senior members of what might be the most murderous criminal enterprise on the face of the earth.

And Varouj Pogharian's left side kept getting worse....

Jaworski was able to buy time from Caycedo, telling him he had to get the correct paperwork to guarantee they wouldn't get caught in Canada. In the meantime, Jaworski said, they should go to Toronto, a cosmopolitan city where two Spanish-speaking men would not stand out.

The stakes were raised now for Jaworski. Caycedo and Pablo Escobar might possibly restrain themselves after losing a planeload of cocaine. But the arrest of Jay was another matter. He was not only Caycedo's most experienced pilot and one of his friends, he was also a blood relative of the wife of Pablo Escobar. Murderous revenge would be necessary for professional and family reasons. Without it, others might do the same. Revenge didn't just satisfy a basic urge. It was also a way of keeping Escobar's workers in line.

Pogharian spoke Spanish fluently but pretended not to understand the language. That way the pilots might loosen up in Spanish around him. Pogharian was an intelligent man, and the strain of feigning ignorance as he listened in on their private conversations was enormous. There was the constant urge to jump in with the right word or phrase when the pilots struggled to explain something to him in broken English. At one point, Pogharian caught himself starting to whistle a

Colombian folk song while shaving, only to stop, horror-struck, and wonder if the pilots in the adjoining hotel room had heard him. Would the whole operation be compromised by one simple tune?

The day after the flight touched down, the pilots were accompanied by Pogharian and McMaster to the Fredericton airport, collecting tickets to Toronto under Pogharian's real name, plus the aliases of Robert Stringer, Jose Hoya, and Juan Lopez.

Pinguino handed over his Colombian passport, keys, a penknife, and Colombian currency to the undercover officers to hold, just in case he was questioned. When Pinguino traveled, he invariably said he was from Venezuela. It attracted less suspicion.

In the airport, they all stood apart, thinking this would make them less noticeable.

Just as they were ready to board their flight to Toronto, a group of soldiers from the nearby Gagetown base walked toward them. Jay spotted them immediately. Back in Colombia, the military was a major part of the battle against the drug barons. When the soldiers kept on walking, Jay relaxed, turned to Pogharian, and winked conspiratorially, as if to say, "We beat them. We left just before the investigators showed up."

The white Lincoln Continental pulled up at Pearson International Airport as the pilots arrived in Toronto. At its steering wheel was yet another undercover officer. But before they would go anywhere, Jay and Pinguino insisted on calling Colombia from a pay phone. Then the Lincoln whisked them to the Chez Marie strip club for a few hours. Drinks, steaks, and more gyrating skin were served up later on the tables of the House of Lancaster, another strip club.

"Hey, Fernando, they like you," the Mounties joked, as the

pilot rewarded one stripper's exertions with crisp new fifty-dollar bills from the $25,000 cash the pilots were carrying.

That and his heavy gold jewelry, including the $10,000 Rolex, had made him a popular customer. Corporal McMaster had to step in to keep the dancer away from Pinguino's heavy 18-karat-gold necklace, which held an ornamental, Buddha-like baby. It had been blessed by a priest and given to the twenty-three-year-old pilot by his mother before one of his flights. Corporal Pogharian also had to cool down Pinguino when he seemed intent on shucking his Mountie escorts to spend some private time with a dancer. At best, this would complicate things. At worst, it might make the Mounties guilty of a procurement charge. No wonder Corporal Pogharian didn't feel so good.

The Colombians were biding time, expecting to be taking a Friday charter to Cartagena, Colombia. On Wednesday, April 5, they were ushered off to Sherway Gardens for a shopping spree, picking up $500 suits, $350 shoes, perfume, a leather jacket, and numerous shirts. Corporal McMaster estimated that Jay alone spent $5,000 over a few hours. He almost spent another $2,000, after spying a picture of an Ultrasuede jump suit in a leather goods catalogue.

Then, as their new clothes were being altered, it was off to Niagara Falls. A cheerful Pinguino spent more than $300 on cheap souvenirs. Among their purchases was a disposable camera, which he used to have their photos taken in front of the falls.

Of the two pilots, Jay was more restrained and quietly charismatic. Somehow the way he carried himself spoke of intelligence. Both pilots were obviously used to being treated with a certain amount of deference as befitted the cream of the cartel fleet. Jay would occasionally be deep in thought as he fixed his eyes on Corporal Pogharian, making the undercover Mountie wonder if he had discovered yet that something was wrong.

"Have you heard from Douglas?" Jay frequently asked, pronouncing the name "Dew-glass."

Meanwhile, Doug Jaworski was on the phone in Montreal, complaining. He told Caycedo that his men were mutinous and wanted to be paid immediately. Because of the plane crash, they feared they would not get a chance at future flights. They were demanding their money now, he lied. Caycedo agreed to free up fifty kilos of cocaine from the shipment for quick sale, to raise cash to calm them down. As Jaworski recalled later, "I made such a stink about it that Caycedo decided to contact two or three other groups that he had to generate some cash. He would negotiate a deal and I would drop it off and receive the money."

The ruse gave police a chance to look at the relationship between cartel groups in Montreal and Toronto. Suddenly, the fifty kilos of cocaine was in a police officer's car and bound for Toronto, where it dovetailed into another undercover operation, called Project Amigo.

Hours after Jaworski complained that he needed $100,000 immediately, there was a knock on a downtown Toronto hotel door. Two strangers handed a pair of undercover officers a box with $95,000. They wanted $100,000, not $95,000, an officer grumbled. Police would speculate that the missing $5,000 was scammed by the Colombians. Now police were running undercover stings and surveillance operations in Toronto and Montreal, while worrying that everything could be blown apart if some busybody in the Maritimes happened upon the crashed Commander and started asking embarrassing questions.

Back in Toronto, Corporal McMaster knew it would take only a call to get a hit squad at the undercover officers' door; in Medellin the cartel had actually placed a bounty on police officers and it had never shown much respect for borders. In the first six months of 1990, some 155 police officers would be murdered in Medellin for interfering with *El Negocio*, The Business. The cost per killing was about $4,000, although it could sometimes be done for considerably less. Jaworski had overheard Caycedo ordering the assassination of Brazilian police officers, and what they would do in Canada was anyone's guess. Clearly, police officers were fair game, just like anyone else who got in the way.

No wonder Corporal Pogharian's left side still hurt.

21/ THE DELIVERY

"Just trust your buddy, okay?"

— Diego Caycedo to Douglas Jaworski.

ON APRIL 4, THE DAY AFTER THE FLIGHT touched down, Doug Jaworski called Diego Caycedo to talk about five exciting "girls" — the code name for the 500 kilos of cocaine flown into New Brunswick. All Caycedo told him was the Montreal-area pager phone number for a contact code-named John. Caycedo was directing cartel underlings like chess pieces, moving huge amounts of money and drugs while releasing precious little information.

Caycedo: Right after you meet John, call me and let me know. I'm gonna move on the other things now... and other people that we got over there.
Jaworski: Well, I'm not gonna meet John until I give him the girls [cocaine], probably.

Caycedo: Yeah, that's what I'm saying. That just meet John and right after you give him the girls, you call me....

Jaworski sounded leery, so Caycedo lectured him on the need to trust his associates in the cartel. "I have another group which is also receiving some. Then I'm gonna talk to three groups that I got, okay? Okay?"

Jaworski: Uh-huh.
Caycedo: Ah, listen. Just trust your buddy, okay?
Jaworski: I love you, but not quite that much.
Caycedo: Same way your buddy trusts you, you gotta trust him.

Jaworski called the pager number and, three minutes later, the man whom Caycedo had code-named John called back. John's true identity was a mystery. Canadian police would come to believe he was really Richard Delgado-Marquez, a broad-shouldered, light-haired, twenty-three-year-old Puerto Rican national who had grown up in Medellin and now lived in the Bronx, New York, close to the cartel's cocaine stockpiles in Queens, New York. But Jaworski had his doubts about his nationality. "I always felt he was Colombian. He had only a birth certificate for proof. The DEA later checked his apartment and found a stack of fifty blank birth certificates."

In the phone conversation, Caycedo also hinted that he had three groups working around Montreal. The police had identified only two of them and even that was a considerable accomplishment. Cartel members overseas were as elusive as smoke, shunning gambling and other street crimes that might attract police attention. Even when they were caught, which was a rarity, they didn't yield much information. They generally did not have much to give, since they were told things only on

168 THE BIG STING

a job-to-job, need-to-know basis. The real thinking was carried on a continent away, in Caycedo's safehouses.

In major drug transactions overseas, a buyer negotiated with a seller, who would verify his credentials. The cocaine then moved from a safehouse to a transportation person whose only job was to hand over the drug. Buyers were always two stages from safehouses holding drugs, and the person delivering the drugs would not even know the location.

And even if cartel workers did know something significant, they usually remained silent. Their loved ones — mothers, brothers, aunts, uncles — were indirect hostages back home in Colombia. To ensure their silence, it was usually enough to say casually over a long-distance phone line, "I saw your sister yesterday and she was very healthy."

Police knew that one cartel group distributed the cocaine that Caycedo was flying into Sorel in January 1989 while the other was in charge of handling the New Brunswick shipment. Caycedo had links to Hell's Angels bikers and the well-established West End Gang. Hell's Angels had accompanied cartel members as they timed the drive from Sorel airport to the nearest police station. They were confident the twenty-two minutes the drive took was plenty of time for a getaway.

The West End Gang began working under the Colombians in cocaine trafficking shortly after the South American criminals started showing up on the streets of Montreal in the early 1980s. Since then, well-established Mafia groups had also learned to coexist with the Colombians in the cocaine trade, leaving much of Montreal's downtown to the newcomers and redirecting their trade to outlying areas. The Cuban traffickers' bloody experience in south Florida had shown the dangers of trying to fight back against the Colombian cartel tide. In return for allowing them in without a war, the Mafia groups got discount wholesale prices on cocaine.

Doug Jaworski was late. He had arranged to meet John at a downtown Howard Johnson's restaurant on St. Catherine Street an hour after their telephone introduction. Jaworski had said he could be recognized by his aviator glasses, gray leather jacket, and blue-green shirt. When he and undercover Mountie Wayne Umansky arrived, they noticed a young Latin man on the pay phone and reasoned it was probably John, calling Jaworski to find out the reason for the delay.

They were only a few minutes late but Jaworski had made his point. A late arrival ensures people are thinking of you well before you make your entrance. Jaworski often arrived late. "It was a good way of showing I was in control," Jaworski later said. "I could show up whenever I wanted."

"John?"

"Daniel?"

With those two words, they sat together in a booth, and the $250-million drug transfer was under way.

Jaworski told John that the "merchandise" was okay, but asked for help raising money to calm the pilots, Pinguino and Jay. John said he would talk with his boss, but, in true cartel fashion, did not indicate who that was.

They agreed on a second meeting at the same location that afternoon. This time Flor Emilse Mery-Correa, a hardened-looking woman in her early thirties, showed up with a Latin man, Fernando William Mendoza-Salazar, who appeared to be in his late twenties. Mery-Correa scarcely acknowledged Jaworski and Umansky. She might once have been beautiful and was still attractive, but she carried herself with a confidence that spoke of business, not sex. She also had the air of someone of importance, which she was. Had she chosen to chat with Jaworski and Umansky, she could have told how she had been flown up from Colombia just for the meeting and how it had been her brother and sister-in-law who had delivered the $95,000 to the undercover police officers in Toronto. Perhaps most significantly, she might have addressed rumors that she was romantically involved with Pablo Escobar. Others at the table ordered beer and cheesecake, but Mery-Correa had nothing. She also said nothing, seeming to scrutinize everything and everyone. "She was there to look out, looking for surveillance, anything," Jaworski later said.

The cartel was something of an equal opportunity employer where women were concerned — a relatively liberal outlook not shared by the Mafia, Chinese triads, or Jamaican posses. The cartel existed primarily to make huge sums of money, not to satisfy macho egos, and its male leaders realized that some women could be as dishonest and ruthless as the men could. Men still had most of the violent, physical jobs, but there was plenty of other work. In the cartel, separate people were often in charge of transportation, safehouses, cars, delivering money, delivering drugs, laundering money, and transporting money out of the country. New arrivals to Canada got the riskiest jobs, such as acting as delivery people for money jobs. If they did well, they moved up to getting cars and putting drugs in cars. The next promotion was running a safehouse. All delivery people in a city often worked out of the same apartment, passing it on much as someone in the foreign service would pass on his or her lodgings.

The most reliable people in a foreign land were put in charge of handling money, since cocaine was far more easily replaced. Money moved from the person who picked it up to a safehouse, to a senior money-mover, who shipped it out of the country in packages or tried to compromise a financial institution to wire-transfer it south.

Almost everyone involved in this network expected to move up and get rich within three to five years, then return to Colombia wealthy enough to retire.

None of the cartel members in the Howard Johnson had

been in Canada long. John had called Mery-Correa in Colombia from Montreal on March 13, 1989, and the next day, she applied for a Canadian visa. At the same time her brother, Albin Geovanny Mery-Correa, and his wife, Beatriz Pelez, applied for Canadian visas in New York. In effect, they had all been transferred.

The conversation at the restaurant soon shifted to the delivery of the cocaine. It was decided that Umansky would deliver a rented van to the Colombians downtown on Drummond Street. He would climb out, and a Colombian would take the wheel and later return the van to the rental agency. There was no sense attracting attention to themselves by upsetting the rental agency. They were international drug traffickers, not petty car thieves.

Four men and a woman sat nearby in the restaurant and watched discreetly. When the Colombians left, so did they. The second team of undercover police officers had not been told the intricacies of the case or who exactly they were following. They shadowed John, Mery-Correa, and Mendoza-Salazar on foot, in cars, and in a helicopter.

Mery-Correa had a jolt that day when she tried to cash two cheques totaling $3,000 at a Bank of Nova Scotia. The teller noticed that the cheques were in Spanish and decided to chat in that language as they waited for the cheques to pass a security clearance. Mery-Correa and John froze when they were asked where they were from, before replying, "Caracas." Like Pinguino, they knew it was safer to say your home was Venezuela rather than Colombia.

The chatty teller was surprised. She had close friends from Venezuela. Wasn't it curious that their accents were different from those of John and Mery-Correa?

Mercifully for Mery-Correa, she didn't press the point and cashed the cheque. As the Colombians left, one of the police surveillance team approached the teller and learned that Mery-

Correa had given a New York address as part of her identification for cashing the cheque.

Meanwhile, Jaworski was back on the phone to Colombia. Caycedo didn't like mysteries. He wanted to know exactly what had gone wrong with the New Brunswick landing.

"Was that a human failure?" Caycedo asked. "What happened? They slipped or what?"

"I don't know. I'll let them tell you about it when they see you."

"You mean, they could have gone back?"

"If they didn't crash, they could have gone back."

"Really, but wasn't the people [another plane] on top of them?"

"They said that, but I never saw anybody."

Jaworski didn't want to increase Caycedo's suspicions by talking about official surveillance, but he could also not afford to sound evasive. He was not lying completely when he went on to say that he needed a break from cartel business.

"I'm worried about my security," he said. "I want to escape for a little while and take a little vacation and maybe come and see you or something, but I'm not gonna stick around here, exactly."

He hoped that this explanation would buy him enough time to be long gone before Caycedo realized he had been stung.

Meanwhile, police were trying to trace the pager number for "John," which they realized could have been rented under a phony name or address. They also tackled the huge task of inserting the cocaine into exhibit bags and replacing 450 kilos of cocaine with brown sugar for the sting. Brown sugar was cheap and had roughly the same weight as cocaine. Tight controls were needed for the job, which was done in an RCMP warehouse in St. Hubert, near Montreal. "Continuity" was needed to make the evidence stand up in court, meaning it had to be accounted for at all times. To ensure this, the cocaine had been accompanied to St. Hubert by Sergeant Umansky, who hadn't had time to shower and change out of his gasoline-drenched work clothes.

The Mounties also had to consider a novel but potentially serious health hazard. The cocaine they had seized was 95 percent pure, meaning it would normally be cut four times before hitting the streets. Gloves and masks were mandatory for officers handling the cocaine during the fourteen-hour job. The twenty-five bales were individually repacked with twenty bricks of plastic-wrapped sugar, each the size of a telephone book, then covered with Styrofoam and fastened with green tape by Mounties working side by side on a makeshift assembly line. A tiny bit of the original narcotic was left in each package so that drug charges could still be laid. Compact police receivers were also inserted so the cocaine could be traced once it was returned to the cartel.

Since the whole operation turned on tiny details, the Mounties had to search for exactly the right tone of tape to seal the bales. Just in case the cocaine was to be delivered to Toronto instead of Montreal, officers there had to be ready also and had already hustled off to buy up every available shade of 3M binding tape they could find.

Jaworski had pushed the Mounties to deliver the real cocaine, not sugar. That way, it could be traced all the way to its final warehouse, netting police a huge haul. Or police could turn the vanful of cocaine over to cartel members, then ram it with an unmarked police car. In a fake investigation of the minor traffic accident, police could enter the van, feign surprise at discovering the cocaine, and make arrests. That scenario would have allowed Jaworski to plead innocence to Caycedo and go on his way, free of commitments to police and the cartel. "It would have been plausible deniability on my part," Jaworski said. "I could say I wasn't at the car wreck. I don't know what happened. They would have been suspicious, but suspicious doesn't get your parents killed."

But both plans meant putting $250 million of almost pure narcotic back in the hands of the cartel with no guarantee of scooping it up later. The car-wreck scenario would also mean an officer would have to lie in court and say he or she was investigating an accident when this was not the truth. That would be perjury and the whole case might be thrown out of court because of it. There was no point having a sting if there were no convictions. Unlike the cartel, the Mounties had to play by strict rules that were written by others. It was too early for Jaworski to bail out.

Darkness had already arrived at 9 p.m. on April 5, when Sergeant Umansky delivered the van of sugar to John at a prearranged downtown corner. The Colombians had wanted to deal with it in two trips, but the Mounties balked, eager to bring the sting to its climax. Some 100 police officers from three surveillance teams were set to track the van, wherever the Colombians drove it.

The final destination remained no more than a guess. Some suspected that, because of its huge cargo, the van would head straight down to New York City. In a big city like Montreal, it was extremely easy to lose a car, and the ultimate Mountie nightmare was that they would blow it all now, exposing their sting and endangering Jaworski while losing their suspects. Canada's biggest drug sting could easily turn into a colossal screw-up.

The van, shaking under the weight of a half ton of sugar, was backed into the garage of a new townhouse in the largely blue-collar, immigrant Little Burgundy district in downtown Montreal. Mounties breathed a huge collective sigh of relief.

"John's got the $450 and everything's fine," Jaworski told Caycedo when he called Colombia at 10:06.

Caycedo replied that he had two groups of workers in Canada who could pay Jaworski the next day, but still did not divulge who they were.

Mery-Correa was on the phone, too. When the shipment was received, she called a number in Queens, New York, written in code in one of John's notebooks.

Then things went quiet on the bugs hidden in the cocaine. Inside the townhouse, John had received a phone call from a woman who must have been his wife. He told her he had been under a good deal of pressure, then they chatted light-heartedly about a woman they knew who had breasts so massive that she needed back surgery. John heard news about a barbecue with a family called the Escobars, and about a recent trip to Disney World and a fish meal his female companion recently enjoyed, with "a shellfish pot that raises the dead, [it was] so tasty."

Around 11:15 p.m., police listening in on the townhouse could hear some activity. It sounded as if a package was being cut. Perhaps a little party was planned. Suddenly, there were alarmed shouts from the house.

"He knows it's sugar," said Pat Akin, the Mounties' Spanish-speaking translator, to others inside the police van.

"Hit it!" responded Inspector Bill Lenton of Montreal.

The Mounties' elite Emergency Response Team smashed through the front door and rushed in. It was a textbook job. Less than a minute later the cartel members were immobilized, with no chance to flee or destroy evidence.

Then a concerned voice came over the police radio: "We've got everybody arrested and they didn't open the packages."

This is the type of thing that puts a lump into a police officer's throat and the brakes on his or her career. Had Akin jumped the gun? She was considered cool under pressure but everyone makes mistakes and maybe she had hurried things.

It's such little things that kill you, whether you are a cop or a cocaine dealer. Caycedo knew that too. That explained the mania for control, the abundance of paranoia, on both sides.

A back bedroom was searched, an opened cocaine package was discovered, and fear dissipated inside the surveillance van. Akin had done her job perfectly. If she had delayed, evidence would have been destroyed. Calls would have been made to Colombia. Jaworski's role would have been discovered.

The Colombians left the townhouse quietly, without a fight, although one had to be dragged from underneath a bed. Mery-Correa had quietly put down the phone when police stormed the kitchen. After the call to New York, she had called Colombia, asking questions about home improvements and her young son's new day care.

"I'll be out in five days," she snarled as police escorted her to jail.

Late on the night of April 5, the phone lines to Jay and Pinguino's rooms in the Constellation Hotel in Toronto were quietly shut off. The pilots had gone to sleep happy in the belief they would soon be home again in Colombia, with $650,000 (U.S.) between them for flying the cocaine north, plus pleasant memories of Niagara Falls, Mississauga shopping malls, rum, strippers, room-service chicken and New York strip steaks, and exciting stories about the chase into New Brunswick and subsequent crash.

Constable Pogharian was in an adjoining room. He could clearly hear the thump of a battering ram knocking open the pilots' door. A key might have been just as effective, but the Mounties didn't want to fumble with latch chains on the inside of the door. Besides, sometimes the smash of a battering ram alarms criminals enough to make them talkative with police. But the two cartel pilots were pros, surrendering quietly without a fight.

Corporal Pogharian could not help feeling a strange sadness for the pilots. They clearly deserved jail, and Pogharian knew and accepted that, but still they had spent the last three days together, posing as friends. There was also the numbness in his left side. Soon, as the stress of the undercover operation subsided, it would vanish.

The police involved experienced the same sort of mixed emotions felt by athletes and actors after giving what they realized was probably the best performance of their careers. There was celebration — even ecstasy — for victory, but also sadness that the drama was over and might never be played so well again. Now they faced the monotony of sorting through mounds of briefs, the gray paper residue of what had seemed impossible four months ago.

And the hope that the whole thing didn't fall apart in court.

22/ FINAL BREAK

"We know everything already."

— Diego Caycedo telephones Montreal the day after the
sting is completed.

THE NEXT MORNING, JAWORSKI PHONED SUSAN
in Florida to tell her that the sting was finally over.

"Please come to Canada," Jaworski later recalled saying.

"No," Susan replied. Instead, she was going to visit her
parents.

Would she go with him to his parents' home in the British
Virgin Islands?

Again Susan refused. She wanted to be with her parents
instead.

"At that instant, I knew the gig was up with the marriage,"
Jaworski later recalled. "I was waiting for it to happen and it
did. It was like the worst possible outcome, but I had finally
completed what I set out to do. Now the threats from Caycedo
would start. Even though I was prepared for it, when it finally
happened, I shed a tear or two. I went through the whole case
thinking, 'I can't deal with this [marriage trouble] right now.

I'll patch that up. I'll fix that up the first minute I have time.' I went through denying there were huge marital problems, knowing that they were there but denying it. I loved her a lot. That just forced me to recognize it."

During the sting, the adrenalin was intoxicating, and police, criminals, and Jaworski had drunk deeply from it. Now, it was a time for hangovers, for assessing damage and the thudding headache that was often real life.

Jaworski never could understand how Susan wanted him to act, or how to control her moods or their relationship. "I was never capable of reading her mind. She was like, 'If you love me, you should know how I feel.' I didn't know how Susan felt unless she told me."

During the sting, Jaworski had been able to get along with Mounties easily on a day-to-day basis. But he often felt lost and hurt when he watched them go home to their families while he returned to his safehouse. "Time and time again, I was left standing alone, to go to an empty apartment."

At noon the day after the sting, Jaworski's cellular phone rang in his room on the twenty-eighth floor of the posh Le Grand Hotel in Montreal. It was Diego Caycedo, calling long distance from Colombia. Sonny had already given him a troubling report about something going wrong in Montreal and Caycedo wanted answers.

"What do you know about it?" Caycedo asked.

"Nothing yet," Jaworski replied. "I got one guy who's acting a bit weird, but I don't know."

Jaworski promised to check it out and talk to John. He said he would change rooms, in case police were on to anything, then call back. It was the last time they would ever speak.

"I was emotional about the marriage problems. I didn't shed a tear for him," Jaworski later said.

Caycedo called back at 2:20 in the afternoon. This time, he was furious.

The phone in Jaworski's room was answered by an

undercover Mountie. Jaworski was already long gone.

"What's happening?" Caycedo asked.

"Okay, we're still waiting for news from T [Toronto], there. From Thomas," the Mountie replied.

There was a short pause, then Caycedo continued, "Who am I talking to?"

"I'm Daniel's [Jaworski's code name] friend, Vic."

"I need Daniel."

"Okay, Daniel's gone out for a few minutes."

"Yeah, you fucking guys are putting out all my people. You've given them in. Aren't you, you fucking motherfucker?"

"Fuck you," the Mountie shot back. "What are you talking about? What are you talking about?"

"Yeah, all my people are in. I already know. You think I don't know nothing? And I have the names who've done it."

Caycedo's message was clear and chilling through his fractured English, as he continued, "Yeah, is somebody making believe is an idiot and we know everything, already."

With that, Caycedo hung up.

There was one final chapter to write in the sting before it could be considered a success. And there was also the task of keeping Jaworski alive so that he could testify in court.

23/ MIAMI HEAT

"You brought the fucking heat, man!"

— Miami drug trafficker catches on.

CORPORAL KEITH MILNER HAD A STRANGE
feeling, as if he were inside a ghost town. He had just stepped
into Jaworski's Fort Lauderdale ranch-style home with its
screened-in swimming pool, elaborate barbecue built into a
brick wall, and shiny gold pebble patio. It spoke of indulgence.
There was a sunken living room, roomy hot tub, and five
bedrooms for what had been just a family of two. Now it was
empty.

"Not bad, eh?" Jaworski said.

They had stopped in so Jaworski could pick up a few
private effects before they attempted yet another sting.

This time they would be working on the cartel's home turf,
fulfilling Jaworski's commitment to the Internal Revenue
Service in south Florida so they would cancel their tax evasion
and money-laundering investigations on his finances.

Milner was uneasy. In accordance with Mountie policy, he wasn't wearing his pistol in a foreign country. He felt a flash of what it must have been like for Jaworski to rely upon others for protection, and the experience wasn't pleasant.

Word of defectors travels quickly in drug circles. But Jaworski insisted on one last, quick visit, so the Mounties found themselves inside the empty house, unarmed.

Roberto Striedinger, the multimillionaire in the old Nixon mansion, was the target of the new sting. Jaworski called the mansion and was told by a servant that Striedinger wasn't in.

"Is there someone else you can call?" IRS agent Michael Lahey asked.

Jaworski mentioned Fruco, the man who had told him the news of Hans Striedinger's death in the Jet-Ski accident.

Jaworski didn't even know Fruco's real name. In drug circles, such information was not necessary. What Jaworski did know was that Fruco was of the old school, frequently sampling his own product, along with liberal swallows of liquor. That made him a potentially dangerous, ultra-paranoid target, even by cartel standards. Jaworski also knew that Fruco was connected with the Colombian Restrepo crime family, who were strong in New York City.

Fruco had seemed likable when Jaworski had met him in Fort Lauderdale before the Canadian sting. In his mid-thirties, Fruco was a bon vivant who spent much time partying on his cabin cruiser. He was also a big leaguer, with access to 100-kilo shipments of cocaine in Montreal that had been smuggled in through ocean liners.

Jaworski had sold Fruco helicopters, which were useful for moving cocaine paste. During one trip to New York City on a helicopter deal involving Fruco, Jaworski had met a man with two black eyes and a bandaged face. The man's job was to collect money from blacks in Queens for crack cocaine. He said he was injured in a car accident but Jaworski later heard that he was really having plastic surgery to hide his identity from police.

It was a big joke in south Florida drug circles when the man was arrested halfway through his plastic surgery. If Jaworski had thought about it, and if he were superstitious, he might have seen this as a forewarning of how hard it was to shed your past and safely walk away.

"Call him," Lahey said.

The voice on the other end of the line was groggy.

"Who is this?" Fruco asked, obviously not recognizing Jaworski.

"Douglas, your old buddy. Don't you remember?"

"Douglas. How are you? Where are you?"

"I'm in town, man, and I'm wondering if you have any work for me. Times are tough and I need the work."

"Meet me at the Japanese restaurant just south of the Dadeland Mall at 7:30 this evening."

If word about Jaworski's cooperation with police had reached the Miami area, then this was a setup. Fruco had Montreal connections.

But Fruco did not appear suspicious when they met. For three hours they chatted, along with Fruco's wife and mother-in-law, as American agents sat nearby, posing as customers. Fruco departed into a waiting BMW, with plans to meet again the next day.

That night, Susan came by to see Jaworski. She had once radiated control and success. Now she looked emotionally drained. Corporal Milner noted she looked "like a rag doll that someone has knocked the stuffing out of."

When Jaworski called Fruco the next day, he was told to meet the Colombian in a motel parking lot on Ocean Drive in downtown Miami. It was a stretch of the street with heavy cartel business investment. Fruco was on his own turf.

Two bodyguards were with Fruco when he cruised up in a

black Jeep Cherokee Limited with gold trim and leather seats.

"You brought the fucking heat, man!" Fruco cursed.

"What the fuck are you talking about?"

"Over there," Fruco said, pointing directly at the joint DEA-IRS surveillance car.

"I didn't bring the goddamn heat. The fucking cops don't follow a money man like me. It's you they're probably following. You brought the fucking heat!"

"We'll talk while we drive and see if they follow us."

The surveillance team's bumbling continued as they almost immediately lost them in traffic. After a frantic search, their fears were calmed when Jaworski was returned by Fruco to the parking lot.

For the next few days, Jaworski tried to reach Fruco on the phone, with no luck. Then finally the man himself answered, but he was well under the influence of his own product. Through his chemically induced haze, Fruco said he wanted to buy a plane. And could Jaworski help him move a car out of Montreal? It was packed with cocaine.

"Of course," Jaworski replied.

If successful, that would mean another $50,000 (U.S.) in reward for Jaworski from American authorities, in addition to the $200,000 for the Canadian sting. He could also draw another potential 25 percent for all assets seized in the new American operation.

But when Jaworski arrived for a restaurant meeting, Fruco was not there.

Two hours later, Jaworski was on the phone to Fruco, trying to sound jovial.

"I'm not coming all the way over there tonight, Douglas," Fruco said. Instead, he invited Jaworski to a luxury private club frequented by the cartel. "We'll have a few drinks and talk."

Things were going downhill fast for police. The club was

dangerous territory. Since it was private, access was restricted and police could not simply wander in and pose as customers. It was also a known hangout for high-level drug movers.

Inside its walls, Fruco was treated with something approaching reverence. With Jaworski was Sergeant Wayne Umansky, who, Jaworski said, would handle the car of cocaine in Montreal.

Fruco said he wanted to see Jaworski on a bridge over the Miami River so that he could give him a $200,000 down payment for the aircraft. But there was something troubling about his tone, especially a secret aside between Fruco and his bodyguard late in the meeting. As they chatted, a hotel valet rushed in and ushered Fruco aside. A car had cruised by so slowly that it had to be police. Fruco left shortly after that.

The next day, Jaworski kept calling Fruco, but couldn't make a connection. Then there was a busy signal. Then no answer. Fruco wasn't taking calls. Jaworski and the unarmed Mounties realized the sting was dead. The American authorities had blown their cover and any potential sting.

For Jaworski, it was a reminder of how precisely Inspector Blackburn had organized the Maritime sting. Before he had approached the police, Jaworski had wondered if the Canadians could handle his case as well as more experienced American officers. Now he had his answer.

24/ COUNTERATTACK

"As much force as necessary."

— Instructions to guerrilla team trying to break cartel pilots
out of Canadian jail.

YORK COUNTY JAIL SITS IN THE CENTER OF
Fredericton, a sleepy city of 45,000, and is just across the street
from the Centennial Building, which holds the New
Brunswick premier's office. Next to the Centennial Building
is St. Dunstan's Church, with the largest Roman Catholic
congregation in Fredericton. To the rear of the jail is Boyce
Market, a popular and busy Saturday-morning shopping spot.
Every day of the week there are plenty of potential bystanders,
in the unlikely event of a breakout attempt.

Aside from metal grates over the windows, the tiny granite
building looks more like an old library than a jail and appears
unchanged from 1840-42, when, according to a historic plaque
on its front wall, the jail was built. Any curious person could
simply walk up and peer inside the fence at prisoners during
exercise times. The overall impression one gets from surveying

York County Jail is that it would be only slightly tougher to break a prisoner out of its stone walls than to rescue a child from a principal's office. Making things even easier is the fact that anyone trying such a jailbreak would not have to worry about armed guards since the guards don't carry guns and, to borrow a joke from Robin Williams, could do little more than shout, "Stop or I'll shout stop again!" Such light security is enough for the jail's usual clientele of shoplifters and drunk drivers, but it must have amused pilots Jay and Pinguino, two of the jail's newest prisoners.

In June 1989, above a bowling alley, Diego Caycedo and Pablo Escobar met with a career criminal connected to political terrorists in Medellin to talk about breaking the pilots out of York County Jail. They built a small-scale mock-up of the jail from photographs and mental notes drawn from visits by the pilots' families. Even if it looked simple, the cartel would leave no details to chance. At the Medellin meeting, an informer would later tell Mounties, it was agreed that they should use "as much force as necessary" to free the pilots.

This opened up a considerable range of possibilities. It also showed that the cartel regarded Canada with no more respect than south Florida or tropical banana republics. Guns for hire connected to the Revolutionary Armed Forces of Colombia (FARC) and M-19 guerrillas were promised close to $1 million between them for the job. Although they had major philosophical and political differences with the right-wing cartel, they shared a common contempt for government institutions like York County Jail.

Such assaults were unheard of in Canada, but in Colombia they had already become routine. In its decade of existence, the cartel had assassinated three Colombian presidential candidates, Supreme Court judges, cabinet ministers, religious workers, police officers, and thousands of others who challenged El Negocio. The cartel also was not afraid of murdering outside Colombia. On January 13, 1987, Enrique Parejo-Gonzalez, former Colombian Minister of Justice, survived three bullets in the head when attacked in Budapest. Parejo-Gonzalez had become ambassador to Hungary in an attempt to save his life, after, as slain Justice Minister Rodrigo Lara-Bonilla's replacement in Colombia, he had extradited ten cartel members to the United States. His crime, in the cartel's eyes, was compounded when he ridiculed the drug barons' offer to pay off Colombia's $13.5-billion national debt in return for freedom from extradition. After the Budapest shooting, Colombian attorney general Carlos Mauro Hoyos Jimenez said, "It is obvious now that no one is safe anywhere in the world against the vengeance of the Mafia."

Violence was particularly high in the fall of 1989, as there was a renewed push for extradition of criminals to the United States. Colombian jails had already proven poor bets to hold them. Clearly, these were not people who would back off when confronted by the chain-link fence around York County Jail.

The team that Pablo Escobar and Diego Caycedo selected for the New Brunswick job had a long history of violent crime, especially bank robberies, stretching as far away as Sweden. Springing someone from jail was not that much different from stealing money from a bank, since both can involve hacking through metal, using an elaborate string of getaway vehicles, and possibly the slaying of innocent victims.

The brown van backed up to York County Jail unnoticed. A generator, hooked to a saw, was started up. It would quickly slice through the chain-link fence that separated Jay and Pinguino from freedom.

If the unarmed guards tried to stop them, the van's occupants could draw on their arsenal of more than a dozen guns, which made a nasty progression from .22 caliber derringer pistols to a Chinese AK-47 assault rifle and an Israeli Uzi 9 mm machine-gun pistol. Tear gas, a grenade, electric stun guns, throwing knives, and machetes augmented the weaponry.

Everyone would flee in the van, then switch to a white 1982 Buick parked nearby at the end of a one-way street. It would be hard for anyone to see into the Buick, since the guerrillas had recently paid to have its side windows tinted at Auto Art and Sound in Saint John. Its driver had said he would soon be driving children and did not want them to get sun in their eyes. He wanted the windshield done too, but he was told that was illegal.

The Buick would be driven four miles out of town to a secluded area, then hidden under a camouflaged tarp. After yet another vehicle change, the team would head toward the New Brunswick-Maine border over the back roads and trails that had carried rum runners six decades before. Their destination was the border town of St. Stephen, New Brunswick, where they planned to cross the St. Croix River in a Zodiak rubber boat they had recently bought for $1,432 cash. They had already scouted the river in rental canoes from a resort lodge in St. Stephen. On the American side, a second team of a dozen cartel workers was waiting with recreational vehicles to rush them to a safehouse in Boston, then to Florida and, finally, on a flight home to Colombia.

The plot's authors had taken great pains to keep a low profile and ensure their planning was exact. The first group of the breakout squad flew into Toronto on July 1. The squad's second half flew into Montreal on July 8. Among them was the team's leader, Julio Cesar Bracho-Sucre. His string of known aliases of Jaird Perez Rodriguez, William Jose Rodriguez, Ricardo Marin, and Alexander Galindo-Escovar was about average for the group, as was his age of forty-four.

They had met in Montreal at a downtown hotel, then

fanned out across the Maritimes and New England in rented cars, scouting escape routes from the jail. So as not to call attention to themselves, they rented vehicles from Prince Edward Island and Halifax. Using false Venezuelan passports, they crossed the border into Boston and New York City, to make sure everything was organized with the members there.

Originally, they had planned to bust the pilots out through the front door of the jail. But they noticed that the jail's lobby had been renovated that summer, after they had constructed their model of the jail. Cutting the fence was a better plan and the optimum time was just as the prisoners' exercise period began. Two of the eight members of the team would get out, packing assault rifles, while a third member hacked through the fence. Bracho-Sucre would walk to a corner of the exercise yard and make eye contact with the pilots to alert them.

And if the pilots did not come along, they would be shot dead. How could anyone who did not want out of jail be trusted by Pablo Escobar?

This was the second time the van had been backed up to the jail. The first attempt had failed when a telephone check alerted them that the team on the American side of the border was not ready.

Another call was made to the team in the U.S., just to be sure they were ready this time. They weren't.

The brown van pulled away again, unnoticed.

The cashier at the convenience store near Edmundston was curious. Latin men are a rarity in New Brunswick, and news of the huge cocaine seizure at Wayman Field back in April had been liberally splashed through the press and on the airwaves. Now, on September 13, these strangers wanted to use the pay phone at her store. But when she peered out the window, she noticed that packages were being transferred between their van and a white Buick. Drugs? Just to be sure, she called the

RCMP, who passed the tip over to the Edmundston city police. Suddenly, after all their meticulous plotting and scheming, five members of the breakout team were bagged because of an alert cashier. They gave up without a fight.

Radio news broadcasts that afternoon played up the arrests. By luck, Bracho-Sucre was in another car and escaped detection. He telephoned Diego Caycedo, apparently to pass on the bad news. Then he pulled his rental van in for gas at a Fredericton Irving station.

The attendant who greeted him had also had a busy day. Richard Duplain's day job was working as a reporter for the Fredericton *Daily Gleaner* and, as fate would have it, that day he had written about the unlikely arrest of the five armed men near Edmundston. Duplain was due to cover a preliminary hearing for the pilots Pinguino and Jay the next day.

He offered the van's passengers apples as part of a promotion for the gas station, but Bracho-Sucre politely declined. Duplain thought this was odd. Didn't everybody like apples? Something about the passengers' clothing somehow also struck him as out of place, although he wasn't quite sure what it was. But the men were pleasant and tipped him a loonie for $10 of gas. Always the reporter, Duplain jotted down their license number as they pulled away.

Minutes later, an off-duty police officer drove in for gas, and Duplain mentioned they might have company from out of town at the pilots' court appearance the next day. He then mentioned Bracho-Sucre's van and passed on the license number.

Thus, the Saint John police were waiting on September 14 when Bracho-Sucre pulled into a Tilden office to renew the van's rental. Two of his companions, who had left the car to use a nearby bank, escaped in a cab. Suddenly, only two members remained at large from the guerrilla squad and not a shot had been fired.

Because of the cashier and reporter, police had arrested some suspicious, heavily armed strangers and amassed a mound of interesting evidence. But what did it all mean? Why exactly did Bracho-Sucre need two derringers, stun guns, maps of Fredericton, Quebec, and Montreal, throwing knives, machetes, lifejackets, two-way portable radios, binoculars, instructions for operating bolt cutters, bottled water, pita bread, camouflage rope, an inflatable boat, a .22 revolver, an assortment of camping gear, and a book on how to tie knots? And why were two sets of directions to St. Stephen written in Spanish on a warranty for a Zodiac boat?

Originally, police assumed that they had stumbled onto an off-load team for another cocaine shipment. Then Sergeant Mark Fleming of the RCMP in Fredericton took a close look at two Venezuelan passports that had been confiscated in the initial arrests. Fleming had worked on the sting that April that had put Pinguino and Jay in jail and had seen the pilots in person. Now, photos of Pinguino and Jay were looking up at him from passports bearing the names Jesus Enrique Rodriguez Colmenares and Antonio Barja Desoroa. Suddenly it all made sense: a cartel breakout plot had just been ruined.

It was a miracle that no one had been injured in the arrests. Even more surprising was the fact that the cartel pilots were still behind bars in tiny, antique York County Jail.

25/ FLIGHT AND FIGHT

"People think we are monsters."

— Member of cartel assault team sent to Canada.

SERGEANT BOB LOWE CALLED JAWORSKI'S parents at their home in the British Virgin Islands and his message was blunt.

"Get out now!" Lowe said. "As soon as you can! Get out now! Get out as fast as you can!" The Jaworskis were told to fly to Toronto immediately, not even to pause in the United States to pick up their winter clothes.

They had decided to stay on in the Caribbean after the sting. There didn't seem to be a threat to them back in April, and their sailing cruise business represented their retirement package.

But things were different now. One of the assault team from the botched New Brunswick jail breakout had talked to police, telling them that Pablo Escobar himself had arranged the murders of someone named Douglas, his wife, and all his family after the escape of the two pilots. As Lowe got hold of the parents, Mounties rushed to Jaworski's safehouse near Hamilton, Ontario. Within half an hour, he had packed his overnight bag and was gone forever.

As they sat in a hotel near Oakville, splitting $80-a-day expense money, Jaworski's parents thought back on recent events in their own lives. In June, there had been a call on their cellular phone from a man with a heavy Spanish accent asking about Doug. The family had always given out their cellular phone number sparingly because of high service fees. The call was traced to Puerto Rico, but the Ottawa office of the RCMP considered it "too sensitive" to pursue it further, fearing some leak within the phone company. Another call from a man with a Spanish-sounding voice had also been placed to Doug at his parents' house, but it couldn't be traced because it was from overseas.

Hit squads weren't the Jaworskis' only worries. What would happen to their house and business in Tortola if they were pulled off the island for good? What was the dollar value of their property? What would they do for a living now? The RCMP were not used to having people in their protection who had sizable assets, and such questions were disturbing for the force as well.

The lunch at the Toronto-area restaurant was supposed to help sort things out. The Mounties were represented by Inspector Don Willett, who had just become head of the Toronto drug squad that summer, becoming Blackburn's boss. Willett had not been part of the thrill of the chase or the sweet triumph of the most successful narcotics sting in Canadian history.

Jaworski had become a major problem for Willett and the Mounties since the heady days of the sting. Just as things should have been winding down, Jaworski was angry again. Now he was balking at testifying at the upcoming trials.

Without him, the cases against the pilots and Montreal distribution team might fall through, making the sting a dangerous and costly waste of time. As a condition of his continued cooperation, Jaworski was demanding absolute guarantees that his parents would be safe and that they would be compensated for any losses they suffered during relocation. To underline his seriousness, Jaworski hired Robert Rueter, a lawyer from the pricey establishment firm Stikeman Elliott, whose legal stable has included the likes of former prime minister John Turner, former finance minister Marc Lalonde, and former ambassador Allan Gotlieb. Rueter had a reputation for civil liberties work, and Jaworski had read about him in a book by RCMP informer Leonard Mitchell and journalist Peter Rehak entitled, *Undercover Agent: How one honest man took on the drug mob — and then the Mounties.*

Willett did not go to the lunch with the intention of making new friends.

"At some point, you've got to look at what's real here," he told the Jaworskis.

Willett saw Jaworski's parents as salt-of-the-earth types. But he felt their son had taken advantage of their good natures. Perhaps they should have a long talk with their boy about his days with the Medellin cartel. They might also ask if he had money stashed away.

"I think you should look at this young man across the table," Willett later recalled saying. "You shouldn't expect the force to assume total responsibility for your well-being."

Willett talked about relocation for the Jaworskis, but only in abstract terms. They could sell their business on their own, and if the price was below what they considered fair market value, they could negotiate to make up the difference with the RCMP.

He noticed the Jaworskis' mood had shifted from congenial to indignant.

"Did you ever think of kidnapping?" the Jaworskis asked, fearful they might be abducted.

Willett later recalled replying that he did not think they would be killed. "If they did take you hostage, it would be for the purpose of getting you to say where he was."

The Jaworskis wanted reassurance, but Willett refused to sugar-coat things. "I can't convince you of what you want to hear."

Things were now decidedly ugly. Doug Jaworski later said, "As far as I was concerned, the RCMP broke their commitment with me and I was about to break my commitment with them. I went fucking wild. It didn't matter. The RCMP wasn't going to budge. They made their position and that was it. I said, 'Okay, fuck you. I'm not going to testify. What are you going to do?'"

The sting should have been in its final, triumphant chapter. Instead, it was under attack from within.

Frank the gofer had another chance at revenge for the profits Jaworski had squeezed him out of on the sales of aircraft and parts to Caycedo.

Now, he was showing a private investigator with strong cartel connections all of Jaworski's old Fort Lauderdale haunts. Frank and the private investigator told Dave — the boss of the man who had the pin rammed through his testicles — about court documents from preliminary court hearings in Canada, saying Jaworski's "name was all over them" and that they knew what he had done. Without going into details, they explained they were trying to settle an old debt.

The Florida private investigator also worked for Eduardo Martinez Romero, a financial wizard accused of laundering some $1.2 billion in drug money for the cartel. Martinez was now due to be extradited from Colombia to the United States and Jaworski heard that he would be called to testify against him. Jaworski had been wire-transferred $2 million from Martinez as payment for an aircraft, although he said he did not know its exact origin.

When Colombian authorities prepared to extradite Martinez in September 1989, the cartel struck back by murdering Pablo Pelaez Gonzalez, the popular former mayor of Medellin. Jaworski did not need to be reminded of what had happened to American Barry Seal, who had also been an informant against the cartel. Seal was tracked down by the cartel and, on February 9, 1989, on the steps of his Baton Rouge halfway house, was confronted by a hit squad and shot dead.

Doug Jaworski's parents had lived in a converted restaurant that sat on stilts over the clear turquoise Caribbean Sea in Tortola. They enjoyed throwing food scraps from their house to a pet red snapper. A barracuda lived under their sailboat, where it dined on chicken bones they fed it. And when evening came, the Jaworskis could relax by watching thirty-pound tarpon leaping out of the floodlit water, seemingly lost in play. Maureen Jaworski had loved to go on walks from their home on the sea, across a bridge and up to a hill of palm and thorn trees overlooking the island and coral reefs.

Maureen and her husband, Reg, returned to the island in the fall of 1989 after six weeks in Canada. The situation with the Mounties had not been resolved but the Jaworskis said they had to keep their business alive.

Maureen Jaworski vowed to continue her daily walks, as they tried to put their worries in the back of their minds. Now that they were back in the islands, there seemed no point hiding, since if the cartel really wanted to find them, it would. If police chiefs in Colombia couldn't protect Supreme Court judges, leading politicians, or even themselves from the cartel's killers, there was little that Maureen and Reg Jaworski could do if Pablo Escobar's men decided to make the two-hour flight to Tortola. Maureen Jaworski kept her regular routine, all the while wondering if somebody was on the island watching their movements, ready to grab her.

What had once been idyllic sailboat cruises were now torture, especially when Spanish-speaking men showed up. Whenever someone signed the boat's guest book and listed his nationality as Colombian, Maureen Jaworski now sat down beside the stranger and gave him the twelfth degree, asking where he was from, what he did for a living, and any other question she could think of, always ready to dash to the cellular phone and call for help.

Reg Jaworski would wonder, in the middle of the night, how easy it would be for someone in a speedboat to race by and lob a bomb under the house, which was highlighted by floodlights, and then speed away, leaving no trace of who did it or exactly what happened.

Meanwhile, in Canada, sharpshooters with M-16 combat rifles looked down from roofs of the historic Fredericton downtown. Other members of a paramilitary security team of RCMP and city police patrolled the area with machine guns, shotguns, and pistols. The separate preliminary hearings of cartel pilots Jay and Pinguino and the guerrilla team that had tried to break them out of York County Jail were under way. Judges were ushered into court for the hearings by armed guards, through private doorways and elevators. When Jay and Pinguino were brought to the courthouse in a police convoy, they were immediately placed in separate cells in the courthouse, with machine-gun-packing police officers standing guard outside. The pilots and breakout team were the focal point of what was described as the strictest security operation in New Brunswick's history. Even the premier had been placed under armed guard shortly after the failed breakout attempt. The ultra-strict security would have seemed laughably paranoid earlier in the month. Now, after the arrest of the paramilitary breakout squad, it seemed a reasonable attempt to control the situation.

One of the assault team, William Jose Rodriguez, answered charges of possession of restricted firearms and altered passports by complaining they were badly treated in jail. Clearly resenting the special treatment, he complained, in halting English, "People think we are monsters. But we want to be treated like other prisoners. We are men like other men."

But Judge J.D. Harper of provincial court scoffed at the notion that these were ordinary prisoners. In a considerable understatement, he dismissed an application that the accused could be safely held in tiny York County Jail while awaiting trial, saying, "I am well aware of a lack of security at the provincial jail."

The actual trials were to take place in nearby Burton because police thought it would be easier to control security at the small courthouse backing onto the Saint John River. Jaworski was due to testify at the pilots' trial, but, on November 13, 1989, the pilots pleaded guilty. Judge David Russell of the Court of Queen's Bench clearly was not moved by the arguments of the lawyers about the characters of Jay and Pinguino: that they had no criminal records, were active volunteers back in Colombia, read Spanish-language Bibles in jail, and that Jay's wife had given birth to a son since the arrests. The judge exceeded the Crown prosecutor's recommendations of eighteen to twenty years, giving them sentences of twenty-two years each, saying, "Obviously you were more than mere mules. You didn't care about hurt, misery, and further crime and violence the sale of this product would bring on the North American market."

The next month, December 1989, there were police sharpshooters armed with M-16 assault rifles on the snow-packed roof of the small courthouse in Burton, New

Brunswick. A convoy of three police trucks transported the guerrilla team from the failed prison bust-out, who were now handcuffed and hobbled with leg irons. Police with submachine guns patrolled the parking lot of the building. Charges in court ominously listed the locales of the plot as "Fredericton and elsewhere in New Brunswick; Calais, Maine, and elsewhere in the United States; and Medellin and elsewhere in the country of Colombia."

The breakout squad members sat glumly and then pleaded "Culpable" to authorities, who still weren't even positive of their correct names, ages, or nationalities. But whoever they were, they were at least in custody and would remain so for quite some time. Judge Harper sentenced them to ten years each for conspiring to commit a jailbreak, suggesting that their crime was so arrogant that it had not even been anticipated by Canadian law makers. "My only regret is that I am limited to the term of ten years in penitentiary. I have not the faintest doubt in my mind that what was planned here and almost succeeded qualified as an example of the worst circumstance under which the offence could be committed and deserving of the maximum punishment." He then continued, "Let us compare, for example, the twenty-two-year sentence passed upon the two Colombian pilots you sought to free and realize that, although the importation of dope is an evil abhorred by all good citizens, they carried no arsenal. They were not prepared to kill, maim, or injure to achieve their end. Their motivation was greed alone."

The guilty pleas meant Doug Jaworski once again did not have to testify.

But there was still the upcoming trial for Flor Mery-Correa and the rest of the cartel distribution team arrested in Montreal. Maybe Rueter could overturn Jaworski's subpoena to testify there. "I didn't want to do any more damage," Jaworski later said. "I wanted to stop the damage and that could be done by quashing the subpoena. It would make it worse for my parents if I testified against the cartel."

And if that failed to get things under control, there was always a flight to Europe....

Then, in mid-January 1990, Maureen Jaworski was alone in the British Virgin Islands. Her husband, Reg, had gone north to comfort his mother after his father's death. The cellular phone rang. Again it was a man with a heavy Spanish accent, wanting to speak with Doug. Again the call was from off the island.

Despite the potential danger, Doug Jaworski's parents said later that they felt a certain pride about their son's coolness under fire. "He just seems to be able to go through these things and come out smelling like a rose. I don't know how," Reg Jaworski said.

Maureen Jaworski agreed. "I don't know how he did it. There's a talent in there somewhere. It should be used."

But they knew the adventure was not over yet. At one point while in Canada, Maureen Jaworski had turned to a Mountie and asked, "If the bad Colombians ever came and kidnapped me, would you come down and find me?"

"Absolutely," was the Mountie's instant reply.

But they both knew the situation was far too complex for any one police officer to sort out.

Unknown to the family, the RCMP had heard of yet another threat. A cartel witness told them that Pablo Escobar "mentioned that after this operation [the jailbreak], he had already organized another group who would get Doug Jaworski, kill his family, his mother, his father, everyone including the canary."

26/ LEGAL LAST RESORT

"My God, I can't believe how much depends on this one person."

— Douglas Jaworski looks at the judge who must decide if his parents are in danger.

MADAME JUSTICE CLAIRE BARRETTE-JONCAS was in an uncomfortable position. In February 1990, she was called upon to decide the fate of Doug Jaworski's parents. The Quebec Court of Appeal judge had been assigned by the Supreme Court of Canada to rule if there was a threat against them.

The case had been referred to her after the Supreme Court of Canada rendered its quickest verdict in history. The top court had sat on February 2, 1990, and given its decision just thirteen days later. Fear of provoking cartel violence meant it had also been the first closed-door hearing for the Supreme Court, in which the names of Jaworski and his family were not even released.

In Barrette-Joncas's courtroom, proceedings again were top

secret. If the cartel knew what was being decided, they would have had even more reason to make a bloody example of the Jaworskis. Jaworski had made it clear that he would not testify at the sting trial unless he was assured that either his parents were safe or their relocation costs would be paid. Any leak of this would have been an invitation for an attack on his parents.

Barrette-Joncas represented the court of last resort for Jaworski. His suit to quash a subpoena calling upon him to testify against the cartel had been dismissed by the Quebec Superior Court on the grounds that the subpoena was valid. It also ruled that the court had no jurisdiction to hear the case because Jaworski's parents lived outside Canada. The Quebec Court of Appeal ruled likewise.

The case that Rueter then pushed to the Supreme Court of Canada was a novel one. He reasoned that, if the state enforced the subpoena calling upon Jaworski to testify while knowing it could kill his parents, this would be an infringement on Jaworski's psychological and emotional integrity. That would contravene guarantees in the Charter of Rights and Freedoms for the right of a person to life, liberty, and security of the person. Rueter hoped to build upon the January 1988 Henry Morgentaler decision, when the top court held that denial of access to abortion was an infringement of a woman's right to security of the person. Rueter argued that the psychological anguish for Jaworski if he was forced to testify while knowing it could spell his parents' deaths would be comparable to the sort of psychological hardship or injury that a woman might suffer as a result of being forced to carry a fetus to term.

Now it was all down to Barrette-Joncas.

Jaworski had heard that she had a reputation for being fair and an extremely hard worker. But he was afraid to make eye contact with her as he stepped into the small courtroom. He had never been in a courtroom before the sting, and as he looked at the judge, he thought, "My God, I can't believe how much depends on this one person. It all comes down to this?"

Jaworski had just flown back to Montreal from a three-week, round-the-world sabbatical that had taken him from skiing on the Vermont-Quebec border to skating the Rideau Canal to Los Angeles, Japan, Korea, Hong Kong, Thailand, and Scandinavia. Now, as he stepped forward, he could see his parents out of the corner of his eye and they looked nervous. So was he.

"How do you tell a judge that there is a threat?" Jaworski later said. "How do you describe a threat? You can tell a judge how you feel about it. You can say, 'Yes, I know these people are dangerous.'"

Senior Mounties argued that Jaworski did not make an issue of his parents' security and compensation until the cocaine-filled plane was in the air. He had, in effect, used the sting as blackmail to push for a deal. If he cared so much about his parents, why didn't he move them himself, then sue the Mounties for costs? The argument infuriated Jaworski, who later said, "I told them a thousand times all throughout this case that I was worried about my family and they just kept patting me on the head and said, 'Be a good boy, we'll take care of it. Don't worry. The RCMP doesn't fuck people like that.'" Jaworski said that his parents continually refused to allow him to move them. They trusted the Mounties, he said.

When Inspector Wayne Blackburn was called to the stand, Jaworski did not anticipate anything special. He had respected Blackburn's thorough planning during the sting and found him a straightforward, honest man. But Blackburn was from a system that does not encourage public dissent, and Blackburn's Mountie superiors looked on as the inspector stepped forward. Then came the big question from Rueter: Did Blackburn personally think Jaworski's parents would be at risk if Doug testified against the cartel? Jaworski was stunned by what he heard. Court records remain sealed so Blackburn's exact words cannot yet be quoted. But the gist was that Blackburn had personal concerns about the safety of Jaworski's parents.

Jaworski was dumbfounded. "He told the truth! It was amazing! It was absolutely amazing. I had a lot of doubt. I was stunned because I felt that he had ruined his career. He did what he morally had to do. I had never seen anything like it."

Blackburn knew there had never been an example of a Canadian family being wiped out by the cartel, but then there had never before been a witness like Jaworski in Canada. There had also never been an attempted jail breakout like the one in Fredericton. That planned attack had failed only because of the cartel's bad luck. The murder of American informer Barry Seal in Baton Rouge showed the cartel would murder people outside Colombia. And they certainly did not shy away from slaughtering innocent family members of their enemies.

Why wouldn't the cartel kidnap Jaworski's parents? That would keep Jaworski off the stand. And the case was also personal, since one of the imprisoned pilots was related to Pablo Escobar's sister and the cartel had been humiliated by the botched breakout attempt. Escobar did not take defeat well; the sole member of the breakout squad who escaped back to Colombia without being arrested was murdered shortly after his arrival home, apparently as punishment for his squad's incompetence. Further inflaming things was the fact that, on the same day the arrests were made in the Montreal sting, police froze $18 million of Escobar's assets in the Banco D'Occidente in Toronto.

It was time for the cartel to reassert itself in bloody fashion, and terror was a proven method of gaining control.

Understandably, Blackburn does not enjoy talking about his time on the witness stand. As he later said in an interview, "Policing in Canada is not easy at the best of times. We deal with people who are conning the RCMP, [who] con police departments, who try to give a worst-case scenario all the time." Blackburn quickly stressed in the interview that he didn't think Jaworski's parents had ever actually been placed at risk by the Mounties. "The problem is, Douglas has put a tremendous amount of pressure on the RCMP, and when people are under pressure, they have to deal with it. Sometimes it's difficult, but everything passes.... People become very cynical sometimes about organizations. The management that I've had here has expected me to tell the truth all the way through."

The Jaworskis were shocked to hear during the case that the RCMP and Drug Enforcement Administration had heard of the second threat against them, the one "including the canary."

This news was withheld from the Jaworskis because, the Mounties argued, it would have needlessly alarmed them. "I just could not believe my ears," Reg Jaworski said. "I could not believe it at all. I just thought, 'My God!'"

Jaworski was in his Toronto-area safehouse when Rueter phoned with Barrette-Joncas's February 26, 1990, decision.

"We won," Rueter said. Not only had they won, Rueter continued, but they had won substantially, receiving immediate protection, court costs for the parents, and compensation for any losses they might suffer by coming under police protection.

Like Blackburn and the Supreme Court, Barrette-Joncas was placed in an impossible position by Doug Jaworski. How could she live with herself if she ruled that Jaworski's parents weren't at risk and then their throats were slashed? As Blackburn later said, "Our justice system is predicated on making sure that the innocent don't become victims of crime. So we were back again to the same circumstances that Douglas put me through when the plane was in the air. It was the same situation that he put the judge in when he brought the civil suit."

But, for all the fear, there was still no record of the cartel killing anyone in Canada. Had Jaworski just exploited the paranoia surrounding his old associates?

Whatever the case, there were just three days to get ready for the Montreal trial and the cartel's legal top gun.

27/ SHOWDOWN WITH SYD

"In the beginning, they thought I was a sleazeball."

— Douglas Jaworski describes the reaction of a jury to his early testimony.

DOUG JAWORSKI'S FIRST EXPERIENCE IN THE trial of the Colombian distribution team nabbed in the Montreal sting was enjoyable, if bizarre. Back in May 1989, Jaworski flew into Montreal for one day for a preliminary hearing. His companions for the flight included his friend Sergeant Wayne Umansky, whose straightforward honesty and self-effacing sense of humor had helped make the sting bearable for Jaworski. Now they wore business suits and Jaworski was where he loved to be: center stage. He stopped in the doorway of the plane, looked at a young flight attendant, smiled, and said, "God, that's what I love about this airline."

"What's that?" she asked.

"The good-looking flight attendants."

She laughed, and when she came around to serve breakfast,

she gestured to Doug as she said to Umansky, "Oh, we love this guy."

As they landed in Montreal, Jaworski looked out the window and saw at least a half dozen green-clad soldiers with M-16 assault rifles.

"What's going on here?" he asked Umansky. "There must be a bomb or something."

"No, I think that's for us."

Since the foiled breakout of the pilots in Fredericton, Jaworski had been a Level 6.5 security risk, which put him .5 below the Pope and U.S. president George Bush but 1.5 above unpopular Canadian prime minister Brian Mulroney. Jaworski later recalled, "The whole plane was starting to hum. They were wondering, 'What the hell's going on?' The flight crew was just going wild. As we taxied to the gate, everybody was trying to figure out who the hell was on the airplane."

A bullet-proof, bomb-proof limousine that's frequently used for Mulroney and visiting foreign dignitaries pulled up. Jaworski found the whole scene unbelievable, as heavily armed police guards met him at the doorway and rushed him into the long, black automobile. He later recalled, with wonder in his voice, "Just before I went out the door, I turned around and waved at the flight attendant. I bet they're still wondering who that was. Their jaws were down to their knees. I thought that was fun."

The limousine is called "the fishbowl" because of the distorted view through its thick, bullet-proof glass, and what Jaworski saw through it was strange but exciting. "We went — sirens, the van, the guys with the machine guns — screaming down through the city, all the way straight to the courthouse. It was just amazing to have all the sirens, going through the city. I thought that was really something."

Sergeant Umansky was a top undercover cop in part because of his ability to blend into situations. Now, Umansky was in his home town of Montreal, riding in the same limousine that carried prime ministers and presidents in parades. People stopped along the street to wave in his direction, on the assumption that someone famous must be inside. Umansky responded to the curtain call.

"It was like a home-town parade for him," Jaworski recalled. "He was waving out the window and people on the street were waving back. He was just as overwhelmed and impressed by the show of force as I was. He looked like a home-coming queen or home-town hero. This was his home town."

But Jaworski would quickly realize the fun was over when, in March 1990, the trial began for Richard Delgado-Marquez, twenty-three, of Bronx, New York (whom Jaworski had known as John), Fernando William Mendoza-Salazar, twenty-seven, of Medellin, and Flor Emilse Mery-Correa, thirty-one, of Chigorodo, Colombia, for conspiracy to import, export, and traffic in cocaine and for possession for the purpose of trafficking. Right up until the trial, Mendoza-Salazar had been known to the court as Carlos Mario Ortega-Gonzales, and authorities would sometimes wonder if the names for the accused were right yet. Also named in the indictment was Diego Caycedo, but Canadian authorities knew chances of his extradition were virtually non-existent.

Because of their nationalities, the cartel owed the accused a defense. "They had responsibility for their people," Jaworski said. "Canadian and American pilots were dispensable. But with people from Colombia, there's the feeling that their families had to be looked after. And that could be for a very long time and expensive."

Rumor had it that Mery-Correa was a girlfriend of none other than Pablo Escobar himself. Certainly, she was a valued worker with considerable responsibility, someone important enough to be flown to Montreal just to receive the $250 million of cocaine. Clearly, her treatment in court would be watched very closely from Medellin.

Aside from protecting high-level workers, the cartel also stood to gain a periscope into Canadian police methods. If they were to lose the case, they could at least get a good idea of what went wrong. Like any efficient business, it constantly strived to improve.

For the public, this was a chance for the first in-depth look at state-of-the-art international cocaine trafficking by the Medellin cartel. And for police, it was a test to see if they had played their half of the game by the rules, even though the opposition could resort to murder in order to win. Authorities can't make criminals feel guilty or stop their trade, but they can at least make them more paranoid.

Courtroom security was unprecedented. Three bodyguards flanked Jaworski whenever he entered the courtroom, and he spent recesses in a room guarded by a police dog and the elite RCMP emergency response team. But according to the defense lawyer Sydney Leithman the protection was all just a big show by the Mounties. Ironically, Leithman sounded a lot like the Mounties when they were before Justice Claire Barrette-Joncas earlier that year. Then they had accused Jaworski of hyping the threat of the cartel to win a sweet-relocation deal for his parents. Now, in Leithman's view, it was paranoia, not the Medellin cartel, that was running out of control in Montreal. Particularly irritating for him was the sight of police on the courtroom rooftops with assault rifles. "Get them off the roof," Leithman barked dismissively and often.

Reports of the enormous security made the trial more exciting and drew more spectators. Among the audience was a trio of men near retirement age who formed Leithman's unofficial fan club, preferring the lawyer's underdog histrionics to afternoon soap operas. There were also visits from a well-dressed gentleman from Miami, said to be a lawyer auditing the performance of Leithman's team.

The very fact that Jaworski was set to be the Crown's star

witness was the result of Leithman's seemingly interminable pretrial procedural delays. These delays had given Jaworski and the Mounties time to settle their dispute regarding security for Jaworski's parents. If Leithman hadn't stalled things, Jaworski would have been forced to perjure himself, commit contempt of court, or flee the country. Now, he was the cartel workers' biggest threat.

The cartel was rumored to be paying Leithman upwards of $1 million. They could not have been impressed with their value for money so far.

Courtroom observers noted that Jaworski showed up for trial looking good, with his Armani and Hugo Boss silk suits and alligator shoes. For his first day in court, he sported a tie from HMS Royal Britannica, which was covered with crown designs, delighting Crown attorney Jacques Malboeuf and announcing with panache that he was now back onside with the prosecutors.

Jaworski later said he did not feel remorse about betraying his old associates, although he avoided looking at the three cartel members in the prisoners' box. They had each had the chance to plead guilty and cut deals of their own. "Everybody is given the opportunity to cooperate with the police," he reasoned. "Their refusal to do so has a lot more to do with their destiny than my decision. I certainly did not feel guilty."

Jaworski had been warned to expect a tough time from Leithman, a courtroom veteran who strutted about with as much righteousness as could be mustered by someone who made a good portion of his living defending Mafia kingpins, cartel drug dealers, and Montreal's Anglo West End Gang. Leithman was a vigorous man in his mid–fifties, and Jaworski was one of the few people in the courtroom who could have afforded his flashy gold watch, signet ring, or heavy bracelet. Some police had a grudging respect for Leithman, who made his name as chief lawyer for mafioso Santos (Frank) Cotroni. If police could get a conviction against Leithman, they could sleep easy, knowing they had done their jobs down to the finest details and that they hadn't locked up an innocent person.

Many others saw Leithman as a rich mouthpiece for the worst of the criminals preying upon society. He was paid great sums to destroy cases that had taken huge amounts of effort and tax dollars to prepare. But they had to respect him as an adversary. Although the Mounties were at home on the streets, the courtroom was Leithman's turf.

Jaworski had been warned that Leithman might try to bait him into saying something prejudicial against the defendants, so that he could force a mistrial. That meant Jaworski had to guard himself from mentioning any crimes for which the accused had not been charged. Delgado-Marquez had talked to Jaworski about plans to pick up cocaine from one of the Sorel flights. What if Leithman asked the contents of their conversations? How could he honestly give an answer without being prejudicial? Jaworski also worried that he might misinterpret the lengthy, complicated questions that Leithman was known to dangle in front of witnesses, like a snare waiting to be sprung. Horror stories were already circulating through the courthouse about a recent case in which an informer perjured himself, then ended up facing charges. What if Jaworski slipped and accidentally did the same thing? If the star witness and informer was suddenly in jail, the sting would be ruined and his life would be in even more extreme danger.

Things got off to a shaky start when a nervous Jaworski waved his arms in a lawyerly way, copying Crown attorney Richard Starck's courtroom speech by using phrases such as "ladies and gentlemen of the jury" and "my learned friend." Jaworski later recalled, "I was nervous because I didn't know what to expect. I just had to go in there and tell the truth. I just did the best that I could. My legs were shaking, and in

Quebec, you have to stand in front of the judge and everybody's looking at you. The whole place was packed and everybody was just staring at me. Talking to twelve people about all of the bad things you did in your life — even though I'm not sorry for anything because it's just the way it turned out — is not a fun job."

He related a story that sounded like a twisted, high-tech Huck Finn adventure, starting with the crimes he committed before he even met Caycedo, like flying planes stuffed with money into Bolivia. After a few days on the stand, Jaworski started to enjoy himself. His answers grew longer, and "because I was telling the truth I was never afraid of contradicting myself." His personality was that of a gracious, accommodating young man when he was questioned by the prosecution team of Jacques Malboeuf, Richard Starck, and RCMP Corporal Dan Paradis. But Leithman triggered something quite opposite. As Jaworski later recalled, "I started liking it. I liked challenging Leithman. I liked being at a disadvantage because I was never allowed to ask him questions. And I liked that because I knew that every once in a while, I would get a chance to fucking drive a stake through his heart." Jaworski later said he constantly fantasized about interrupting the lawyer to ask publicly, "Who paid you? How much was it?"

Part of the reason Jaworski loosened up on the stand was that he sensed that the mood of the jury was shifting, and that they enjoyed and appreciated hearing of his role in the sting. "In the beginning, they thought I was a sleazeball. I could tell by the looks on their faces. They were just listening to this shit, and then after a while, they were starting to laugh a little bit and they were starting to smile at me and they were nodding their heads in agreement with the things that I had done and they were going, 'Yeah, go for it.'"

Jaworski claimed he was actually paid only $300,000 to $400,000 (U.S.) from the cartel, a figure Leithman ridiculed as unrealistically low. And Jaworski admitted he had asked for a cut of all assets he helped police seize but was refused. "In the U.S., I know they pay up to 25 percent of the value of the cash or product seized." But as for the $200,000 he was paid by the Mounties, Jaworski insisted he also worked hard for it and took huge risks. "Going to Colombia undercover for the police in February is not the best way to reach retirement age."

When the $200,000 figure was quoted widely in newspapers, Mountie switchboards lit up with potential informers. It was as if every organized criminal in the country had a sudden attack of conscience.

Finally, Jaworski breathed a big sigh of relief when told he could leave the stand on April 2, 1990 — a year less a day after the Fredericton area flight touched down. He picked up his six volumes of wiretap transcripts and was escorted from the courtroom by his three RCMP bodyguards. He was later pleased to hear that his friend, Sergeant Wayne Umansky, was as unflappable on the stand under Leithman's questioning as he was on the street with dangerous criminals. Umansky has a reputation for painstakingly complete notes, and he was able to weather Leithman's onslaught with workmanlike ease. News of Umansky's performance did not surprise Jaworski. "You couldn't throw a rock at the guy. You can throw a rock at a glass house but he was solid as a stone himself."

Leithman wound up his remarks with a full-bore attack on Jaworski's credibility, labeling him a liar and a "tarnished and paid witness," whose testimony could be believed only when supported independently. Jaworski was a streetwise, "flippant, arrogant, and insulting" man with "a giant-sized ego" who remembered details of the cartel only when it suited his purpose.

Then Leithman issued a challenge for the prosecution

team. For all of the hundreds of telephone and pager numbers Starck had tracked down, could they produce one — just one — that directly linked the defendants to Diego Caycedo?

Leithman's summation was on a Friday, and Starck was due to present the Crown's final arguments the following Monday. On Sunday afternoon, Leithman's challenge gnawed at Starck, who hates even microscopic holes in arguments. None of the half dozen numbers Jaworski had used to call Caycedo showed up in date books seized in the defendants' car and townhouse. Another aspect of the trial was also troubling. Someone named "Mauricio" was listed in Delgado-Marquez's notebook, but Delgado-Marquez had said he did not know who this was. Under the name Mauricio was what was apparently a birthdate — 63-16-09. Mauricio was a nickname for Caycedo. What, if anything, was the connection? Hadn't Jaworski told him that the cartel sometimes uses a code in which five is added to every second digit of a series of numbers, starting at the right? Starck tried it out with 63-16-09 and came up with 68-21-14. Suddenly he was ecstatic. The numbers 68-21-14 were the last six numbers of one of Caycedo's phone numbers in Medellin. The first digit for all Medellin numbers was 2, so it was not necessary to include that in the code.

The next day Starck produced a felt marker and large sheet of paper and worked out the code for the jury. Then Starck reminded them that this was the same number that Jaworski called twenty-four times as he and Caycedo planned the cocaine shipment to New Brunswick. The bombshell could not have come at a later — or better — time for the Crown.

Leithman had been given his direct link between his client and Diego Caycedo. The defense lawyer was caught in the trap he had set for Starck.

Shifting his focus to Diego Caycedo, Starck told the jury that they should not downplay his significance just because he was believed to be only thirty-six years old. Starck called

Jaworski's old associate the Donald Trump of the cocaine trade as he argued that success and responsibility can be achieved at an early age. The defense had scoffed at the idea that a twenty-three-year-old like Delgado-Marquez could have been in charge of the cartel's Montreal end of a $250-million cocaine delivery. "There is no correlation between age and competence," Starck countered. "You can be good without being old."

He also swept aside protests by Flor Emilse Mery-Correa that she was only in Montreal to visit her boyfriend, Delgado-Marquez. Mery-Correa was an attractive woman, but not someone easily cast in the role of a dewy-eyed, hopeless romantic. Perhaps for this reason, she was the only defendant kept off the witness stand and shielded from cross-examination. She had sobbed frequently in front of the jurors, but when they were out of the room, her face turned cold and hard. Starck noted she called New York shortly after the delivery, then asked the jury, "How did Flor know how to call this number? It is a code.... For someone who knew nothing it certainly was a lucky shot in the dark."

Despite the arguments, the jury clearly had troubles reaching a verdict. Fourteen days passed and still nothing. What more could they want? Just forcing such a long deliberation was a triumph of sorts for Leithman, who had been faced with a seemingly airtight police case. After all the work of the sting, were the accused about to walk free? The answer would come on the fifteenth day of deliberations, when the jury finally returned.

The accused had been laughing moments before the verdict was delivered. They turned stone-faced when the decision was finally announced; all three were found guilty of possession of cocaine for the purpose of trafficking and conspiracy to traffic cocaine.

Lori MacDonald, the RCMP tape technician, later recalled

some members of the prosecution team crying tears of relief. Some 1,300 Canadian and American officials — including 300 Mounties or Mountie staff — had been involved from three Canadian provinces, and each could have potentially ruined the case and gotten someone killed with a security lapse. The goal at the onset of the case was to target and dismantle as much of the cartel's distribution system as possible. With the verdicts, they had finally succeeded.

Justice Jacques Ducros knew the decision was being closely watched in Medellin and said he wanted to deliver a "strong and clear message" to drug smugglers, letting them know they could not expect lenient treatment in Canada's courts. Delgado-Marquez's sentence was twenty-five years, which, with the time he had already served, was the longest cocaine trafficking sentence in Canadian history. Mendoza-Salazar got twenty-two years, and Mery-Correa eighteen. They had all gambled and lost, with Delgado-Marquez and Mendoza-Salazar earlier turning down plea-bargain deals of eighteen and ten years. Mery-Correa had been so confident she refused even to entertain a deal. Leithman seemed to think that he could use the other two as leverage to let Mery-Correa go free. Obviously, he was wrong. Now the dangerous people funding the defense had yet another reason to be upset with Leithman.

When the verdicts came in, Jaworski was far from the Palais de Justice: "I heard it on my voice-mail system. I was on my boat, out in the middle of the Atlantic. I was just happy it was over."

Jaworski had liked Caycedo, but said he felt no guilt about turning against him. "If he was that good a friend, he would not have tried to have me shot, would he?"

Naturally, the sentences were appealed. But if Leithman was starting to feel he was losing control of his clients and the courtroom, it was understandable. He and Douglas Jaworski had more in common than either would like to admit. They both thought they could flirt with murderous criminals, make a lot of money, then walk away. Jaworski now knew this was impossible and lived under police protection in a secret location.

But Syd Leithman was still in town and everybody knew where to find him.

28/ MURDEROUS LAST CHAPTER

"How are you doing?"
"I'm alive, aren't I?"

— Douglas Jaworski meets an old friend from the Mounties.

WHEN THE MONTREAL STING ENDED, authorities pulled together a number of loose ends. First was the New York district court trial of Ron Whitaker, one of Sonny's Albany airport team. It had been called a "dry conspiracy," since authorities uncovered a plot to distribute cocaine but none of the narcotic. In December 1990, Whitaker was sentenced to 17 1/2 years but his co-defendant, Sonny, simply walked away from charges. Sonny, the man with the dark eyes and lifetime of secrets, was charged under his real name of Floyd Vaughn and court records also listed his alias of William Robinson. Sonny promised to cooperate with the Drug Enforcement Administration, then went out to buy a hamburger, and never returned. His abandoned Buick was later found in North Carolina.

Jaworski spent much of his time after the sting trying to relax. He traveled a lot, visiting a dozen countries in February 1990. He spent the rest of the time settling into a new life and a new identity, minus his former wife, Susan, and airplane business. Aside from his parents, he was roundly condemned by his relatives. Infighting and suspicion inside his family forced his parents to move once again, this time to keep their address secret from a family member they suspected was too close to cartel lawyer Sydney Leithman.

Officially losing his name did not bother Douglas Jaworski, since his grandfather had changed his name too when he moved from the Ukraine to North America in 1917. He too was adaptable.

As Jaworski changed his identity and his life, the cartel was pushing violence to new heights in Colombia. There were 3,377 murders in Medellin in the first half of 1990; by comparison, Toronto residents had been alarmed when that city's murder rate hit a record of sixty in 1989. Huge as the sting was, cocaine was still readily available on Canadian streets and the heavy supply meant dropping prices. And the cartel was obviously not chastened about working in Canada. As the case called Project Amigo was due to go to court in Toronto in the spring of 1991, there was nervous talk that a cartel hit squad was in the city.

Doug Jaworski remained in limbo as he waited for a final Canadian court appearance to conclude. Then, in October 1990, he arrived in Montreal again for the trial of pilot Diego Jose Ganuza. In a sense it was like a school or team reunion, one last get-together for people who had shared an intense, pivotal experience and then moved on with their separate lives. When he met Lori MacDonald, she noticed he was not in his normal bubbly mood. When she asked, "How are you doing?" he replied simply, "I'm alive, aren't I?"

Things had changed for MacDonald, too, since the heady

days of the first trial. Immediately after that case ended, she had quit the RCMP's civilian staff and now planned to become a police officer herself. Like many involved in the case, she had experienced mixed emotions after the trial ended. "That was the biggest and the best case ever. Now, it's almost like withdrawal."

Ganuza's trial dragged into the spring of 1991, and this time there was no horde of reporters and few courtroom gawkers. The giddy fun was gone and all that was left was tight security inside the courthouse and the ugly rancor between Jaworski and defense lawyer Sydney Leithman, who was representing Ganuza. Leithman had cost Jaworski his chance to slip away after the sting was completed. If Leithman had counselled the Montreal defendants to plea bargain and avoid a trial, Jaworski would have been spared the dangerous exposure of testifying in court. Maybe his betrayal of Caycedo would not have been exposed so completely. Perhaps his parents would have been spared the scare of fleeing their home.

On the other hand, Jaworski might have hurt Leithman even more badly. The lawyer was rumored to have made grandiose promises to the cartel. Now, they seemed like lies.

Ironically, Ganuza would have been safe altogether, had he trusted his instincts. He once told Jaworski that he suspected the young Canadian worked for the American Drug Enforcement Administration. Now Jaworski did not even look at Ganuza, who spent much of his time in the defendant's box with a faraway look on his face.

The case was about Diego Jose Ganuza's future, but it often seemed like nothing more than an ugly spitting match between Jaworski and Leithman, who seemed to bring out the worst in each other. Leithman clearly could not stand the sight of Jaworski on the witness stand, wearing his silk business suit with a Canadian flag pinned over his heart. Jaworski now also wore a Mickey Mouse watch and had a pencil jauntily tucked behind his right ear.

Leithman had once seemed the personification of control in a courtroom. He had a considerable stock of tricks to draw from, gathered since the days in the early 1960s when he was a champion of what, in an interview with the Montreal *Gazette*, he called the "gambling cases [and] the whorehouse cases." If he could not win on evidence, Leithman had previously given the impression he could still win on a technicality -- a perjured witness, a faulty search warrant, perhaps even a corrupt member of the legal system. If he asked four stupid questions in a row, savvy courtroom observers would not think that he was in trouble. The presumed reason would be that he wanted to lower the witness's guard for his fifth question, which would be a killer. His performances might not be pretty, but Leithman was in control and somehow would find a way.

For the Ganuza trial, Leithman acted as though everyone was against him, which appeared at least on the surface to be a fairly accurate description. His aura of control seemed to be fading. He constantly walked over to Ganuza, trying to reassure him that he was leading up to something big, something that would leave the Crown's case in tatters. But, when he walked away from the pilot, neither looked convinced.

Once again, prosecutor Richard Starck was cool in court. He had instructed Jaworski to be civil. Jaworski would cooperate to a point, then would momentarily lose control, and give in to the temptation to needle Leithman by calling him "Syd" or "pal." After one, "pal," Leithman wailed, "Your Honor, could we please advise the witness that I am not his pal. I don't want to be his pal."

During the Ganuza trial, Jaworski considered warning Leithman that he might be in danger. He also openly predicted the lawyer could be setting himself up for trouble from his growing clientele of cartel workers. If the rumors that Leithman had been paid more than $1 million from the drug barons were true, then the criminal lawyer was making some dangerous people extremely unhappy. Other courtroom stories circulating through the Montreal courthouse were that Leithman had been asked to refund money to the cartel and that he had balked. One version even had Leithman threatening to talk to police. A Mountie warned Jaworski to keep his comments about danger to himself. Leithman would take such a warning from Jaworski as a threat and use it against him. Besides, Leithman was no novice and must have known, as well as anyone, who he was defending. He had been in Colombia in late spring of 1991 and appeared pleased by his trip.

Just as Jaworski was winding up his testimony in the Ganuza trial in April 1991, a ship sank off the coast of Newfoundland containing an estimated 1,500 kilograms of cocaine — three times the Wayman Field haul. And a week after that, police in Montreal seized 540 kilograms of cocaine at Mirabel Airport, but no arrests were made. The Montreal case involving Jaworski remained the largest narcotics sting in Canada's history, but the cartel was starting to look vulnerable.

Leithman was riding alone in his black Saab convertible at 6:48 on the morning of May 13, 1991. He was just a minute from his home in the Town of Mount Royal, in Montreal, heading to his office to present final arguments for the Ganuza trial that morning. His hopes seemed to be riding on somehow proving that Ganuza was extradited from Florida on a different charge than the one for which he was now being tried. Despite all of his tactics, the trial had been going poorly. Something strong and dramatic was needed to save it.

Suddenly, a car cut Leithman off at a stoplight at the corner of Rockland Road and Monmouth Avenue. Perhaps Leithman didn't see the young man walking toward him from near a telephone booth as he pulled out a .45 automatic pistol. The shots that followed came slowly, accurately, and professionally, until the gunman was leaning right into the convertible. A driver behind the Saab watched in horror but was ignored by the gunman, as Leithman slumped over in the driver's seat. Leithman, the man who had ridiculed tight courtroom security, was killed instantly. As a final, apparently anti-Semitic flourish, a bag of smoked meat was tossed onto the body.

Who would do such a thing? At the time of his death, Leithman had been adjusting his client list to devote his time exclusively to clients who were allegedly connected to the cartel. Leithman represented a number of different Colombian groups inside Montreal, not all of whom got along with each other. There was speculation that, by this time, his old client Caycedo might have fallen from power, in part because of the Jaworski debacle, but this remained nothing but speculation.

For his part, Jaworski had no doubt it was the cartel who ordered the lawyer's murder. "I'm just surprised that it took so long," Jaworski said the day of the killing. "Usually, they were more prompt. He got paid to deliver and he couldn't deliver. It's like a show of force. The cartel seems to be flexing its muscle."

Until the sting and the subsequent attempted raid on the York County Jail, many senior police officers did not even believe the cartel would send hit teams into Canada. Suddenly, the caution shown by Justice Claire Barrette-Joncas and Inspector Wayne Blackburn seemed reasonable, not paranoid. And the cartel didn't look so vulnerable or foolish any more.

"This is a whole new league that you're going to have to adjust to," Jaworski said in an interview the day of Leithman's murder. "I guess this vindicates Blackburn and Barrette-Joncas."

During the last few days of Leithman's life, his old adversary, Doug Jaworski, seemed finally to be getting his own life under control. Shortly before the killing, he had achieved a triumph of sorts. Some friends took bets that he would not live to his thirtieth birthday. He beat those odds in March 1991 and, at his birthday party, was presented with a cake capped with a model airplane crash-landed into the icing.

Back when he made his first, tentative approach to the RCMP at Pearson International Airport in 1988, Jaworski was not launching a crusade against drugs; he was just trying to bail himself out of trouble. For that, he did a solid job and was well paid with $200,000 of taxpayers' money. Aside from the Canadian cases, his evidence helped secure a conviction of money-launderer Eduardo Martinez Romero. He also helped American authorities move against Roberto Striedinger, whom they used as leverage against former Panamanian strongman Manuel Noriega. But Jaworski laughed at the notion of also helping German authorities against Striedinger, unless they paid him $1 million. They refused.

Despite his self-serving motives, police credit Jaworski with showing that huge cocaine flights directly into Canada from Colombia are a reality. The Mounties have also been shown that the cartel can be beaten, if a real effort is made. The Leithman murder is taken by some top police as an indication that the cartel plays for high stakes here, just as it does in all its other places of business.

Jaworski has seen both sides in the drug trade and has high regard for the skills — and honesty — of officers like Inspector Wayne Blackburn, Sergeant Guy Quintal, Sergeant Wayne Umansky, Corporal Wayne Milner, Sergeant Bob Lowe, and Staff Sergeant Allan MacDonald. The problem is not a lack of talent. Quintal argues that the Jaworski case also shows that it costs money to fight international drug traffickers in a meaningful way. Others in the force agree, saying it's ridiculous to expect to deliver champagne cases on beer budgets. During Jaworski's last trial, the Ganuza prosecution, Mounties passed around a Toronto Sun article by Lee Lamothe quoting RCMP Chief Superintendent Richard Dickins of Toronto as saying that investigations into the Mafia and the cartel are suffering because police forces are short of cash. If Jaworski approached the force at that time, Dickens said, "We would have difficulty accepting his offer.... Some high-level informants are backing away from us." Meanwhile, other Mounties grumbled privately that they had been forced either to reject major informers or to send them south to American authorities who could afford to pursue cases. Some officers go so far as to say, privately, that drugs should be legalized and taxed, with more money channeled toward the treatment of addicts.

The Jaworski case also highlights flaws in how criminal assets are handled. The sting cost the RCMP massive amounts of overtime, but all money raised from the three seized airplanes and the cash did not go back to police but to the Treasury Board, another branch of the federal government. Some members of the force look enviously at the system employed by the Drug Enforcement Administration in the United States, in which seized assets up to the cost of handling the case are returned to the DEA, with the rest going to Washington. That way, authorities can afford to handle major-league cases while taxpayers are not overburdened with bills from the war on drugs. Ottawa's Bill C-61, which theoretically allows authorities to confiscate proceeds of crime, is generally considered toothless and unworkable.

Where will Doug Jaworski go, after the cases and the limelight have faded? Will his sharp brain enable him to invent a new life, far from cartel revenge? Or will it land him in another intricate mess that will take 1,300 officials to extricate him from? If Jaworski survives the next few years, odds are good he will live a lengthy life. His worst enemies remain his ego and his curiosity, and they are formidable foes.

For his part, Jaworski said he regrets getting involved with the cartel. "The cost of getting involved is just overwhelming. Look at me. I sold these guys planes and look what it did to me." But he refuses to say he's ashamed or afraid. "When I think about it, I think, 'My God, look what I've accomplished.' I'm amazed that I was able to accomplish that much. Whether it's good or bad, a lot of things have happened because of what I did, and I'm proud of it."

Even Jaworski's friends in the Mounties suspect he has a cache of money squirreled away, so that he will never have to work again. His critics say that, if he is truly repentant, he should direct money made while with the cartel toward charity. Jaworski says he's happy to escape the cartel, not because he feels guilt but because of the crushing paranoia. "The paranoia in the cartel is just brutal. Imagine you're Diego Caycedo, and you have at least an entire police force in Colombia looking for you — and the army too? He can't even go to a restaurant. That's why we always had to have food brought in. I don't think I'm a prisoner at all. I wouldn't go set up a household in Fort Lauderdale again but I think the RCMP has given me a great opportunity.

"Caycedo can't trust anybody. He thought I was his pal. The fact that there are people like Inspector Wayne Blackburn in this world causes Caycedo to lose sleep. The paranoia has a real effect on him. They're all paranoid. Looking back, Milner was correct. Turning to the Mounties was the right course to follow."

On June 19, 1991, Pablo Escobar turned himself in to Colombian authorities, making pious pronouncements about "submitting to justice" and "contributing to peace in Colombia." By doing so, he was also avoiding the seemingly inevitable alternatives of being shot by rivals or captured by authorities. The billionaire's wealth meant he was able to cut a particularly sweet deal. He gained freedom from extradition to the United States, and despite his grisly record, some reports said he might be freed within five years. His prison, a reconverted treatment center for drug addicts, offered a panoramic hilltop view of his old home town of Envigado near Medellin. The prisoner was allowed to handpick his own guards and given freedom to equip the room with whatever comforts he could afford, including female companionship and communications equipment such as fax machines to direct his operations. In effect, the state became his bodyguard.

As Escobar settled into his new home, police in Canada investigated what they feared to be a rare and major security breach. One of the officers who had guarded Jaworski during his trial had abruptly faxed in his resignation and left the country, and now the Mounties feared he had shared a bed and secrets with a cartel kingpin in Montreal nicknamed "The Godmother."

Meanwhile, Doug Jaworski the chameleon says he's confident he can control himself and safely blend into new, non-criminal surroundings.

His survival depends upon it.

GLOSSARY OF CARTEL SLANG

All the way up — New York City
Another guy like me — pilot
Big piece — JetStar executive jet
Car — aircraft
Daniel — Doug Jaworski
Daniel's place — Canada
Dollars — kilos
Driver — pilot
Driving — flying
Exercise — practise flying
50 - 60 bucks — $50,000 - $60,000
East, to the right, where your friends are — Montreal
Echo to whisky — east to west
Enclyopedia — counterfeit passport and support documents
First floor — low altitude
Food — fuel
Ginger — St. Kitts
God — Diego Caycedo
Hotel — Fixed base aircraft operation
Joseph — Fausto Caycedo, Diego's younger brother
Joseph's old beep — Fausto Caycedo's old pager number
Joseph's place, Joseph's house — United States
Little one — small aircraft
Main place — Toronto Pearson International Airport
Mario's place — Montreal
Matricula — registrations for JetStar
Merchandise — cocaine
Mom — Montreal
Other thing — seizure of Commander 980 by U.S. Customs

Peter, Pablo, The Pope — Pablo Escobar
Piece — aircraft
Pig pen — jail
Product — cocaine
Queen — King Air aircraft
Restaurant — refueling facility
T — Toronto
Thomas — Toronto
Thomas' place — Toronto
206 — Cessna 206 Skywagon
Very bad for vacation — very bad for smuggling
Wash the truck — burn the airplane to destroy evidence

INDEX